ENGLISH
FOR EVERYONE

COURSE BOOK LEVEL 1

BUSINESS ENGLISH

FREE AUDIO
website and app
www.dkefe.com

Author

Victoria Boobyer is a freelance writer, presenter, and teacher trainer with a background in English-language teaching and teacher management. She has a keen interest in the use of graded readers and the sound pedagogical use of technology in teaching.

Course consultant

Tim Bowen has taught English and trained teachers in more than 30 countries worldwide. He is the co-author of works on pronunciation teaching and language-teaching methodology, and author of numerous books for English-language teachers. He is currently a freelance materials writer, editor, and translator. He is a member of the Chartered Institute of Linguists.

Language consultant

Professor Susan Barduhn is an experienced English-language teacher, teacher trainer, and author, who has contributed to numerous publications. In addition to directing English-language courses in at least four different continents, she has been President of the International Association of Teachers of English as a Foreign Language, and an adviser to the British Council and the US State Department. She is currently a Professor at the School of International Training in Vermont, USA.

ENGLISH
FOR EVERYONE

COURSE BOOK **LEVEL** 1

BUSINESS ENGLISH

Aa

Project Editors Lili Bryant, Laura Sandford
Art Editors Chrissy Barnard, Paul Drislane, Michelle Staples
Editor Ben Ffrancon Davies
Editorial Assistants Sarah Edwards, Helen Leech
Illustrators Edwood Burn, Michael Parkin, Gus Scott
Managing Editor Daniel Mills
Managing Art Editor Anna Hall
Audio Recording Manager Christine Stroyan
Jacket Designer Ira Sharma
Jacket Editor Claire Gell
Managing Jacket Editor Saloni Singh
Jacket Design Development Manager Sophia MTT
Producer, Pre-production Andy Hilliard
Producer Mary Slater

First published in Great Britain in 2017 by
Dorling Kindersley Limited
80 Strand, London, WC2R 0RL

Copyright © 2017 Dorling Kindersley Limited
A Penguin Random House Company
10 8 6 4 2 1 3 5 7 9
001–289763–Jan/2017

A CIP catalogue record for this book
is available from the British Library.
ISBN: 978-0-2412-4234-6

Printed and bound in China

A WORLD OF IDEAS:
SEE ALL THERE IS TO KNOW

www.dk.com

Contents

How the course works

English for Everyone is designed for people who want to teach themselves the English language. The Business English edition covers essential English phrases and constructions for a wide range of common business scenarios. Unlike other courses, *English for Everyone* uses images and graphics in all its learning and practice, to help you understand and remember as easily as possible. The best way to learn is to work through the book in order, making full use of the audio available on the website and app. Turn to the practice book at the end of each unit to reinforce your learning with additional exercises.

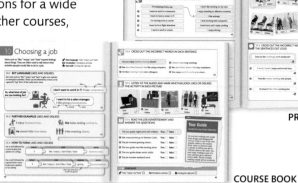

PRACTICE BOOK

COURSE BOOK

Unit number The book is divided into units. The unit number helps you keep track of your progress.

Learning points Every unit begins with a summary of the key learning points.

Modules Each unit is broken down into modules, which should be done in order. You can take a break from learning after completing any module.

Language learning Modules with colored backgrounds teach new language points. Study these carefully before moving on to the exercises.

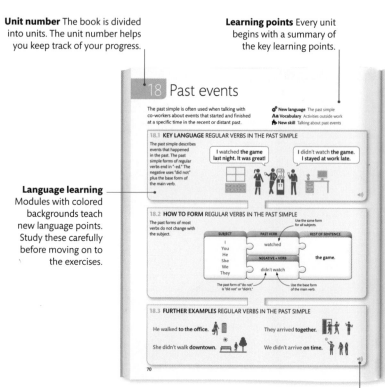

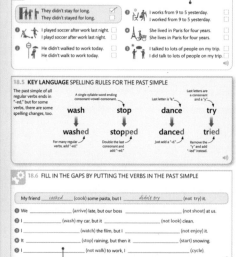

Audio support Most modules are supported by audio recordings to help you improve your speaking and listening skills.

Exercises Modules with white backgrounds contain exercises that help you practice your new skills to reinforce learning.

FREE AUDIO
website and app
www.dkefe.com

8

Language modules

New language is shown in the context of common business scenarios. Each learning module introduces appropriate English for a particular situation, as well as general points of English language to improve your overall fluency.

Module number Every module is identified with a unique number, so you can track your progress and easily locate any related audio.

Module heading The teaching topic appears here, along with a brief introduction.

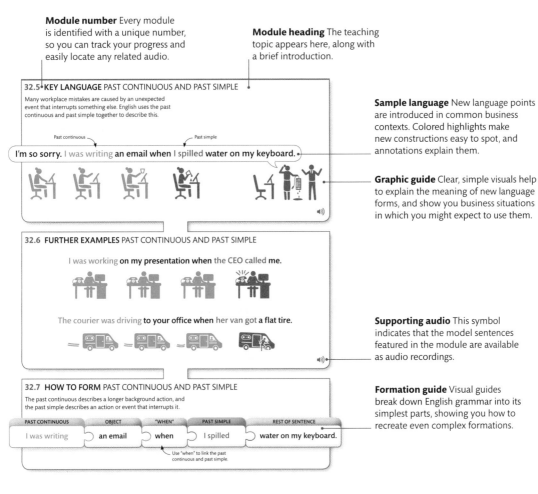

32.5 KEY LANGUAGE PAST CONTINUOUS AND PAST SIMPLE

Many workplace mistakes are caused by an unexpected event that interrupts something else. English uses the past continuous and past simple together to describe this.

Past continuous

Past simple

I'm so sorry. I was writing an email when I spilled water on my keyboard.

Sample language New language points are introduced in common business contexts. Colored highlights make new constructions easy to spot, and annotations explain them.

Graphic guide Clear, simple visuals help to explain the meaning of new language forms, and show you business situations in which you might expect to use them.

32.6 FURTHER EXAMPLES PAST CONTINUOUS AND PAST SIMPLE

I was working on my presentation when the CEO called me.

The courier was driving to your office when her van got a flat tire.

Supporting audio This symbol indicates that the model sentences featured in the module are available as audio recordings.

32.7 HOW TO FORM PAST CONTINUOUS AND PAST SIMPLE

The past continuous describes a longer background action, and the past simple describes an action or event that interrupts it.

PAST CONTINUOUS	OBJECT	"WHEN"	PAST SIMPLE	REST OF SENTENCE
I was writing	an email	when	I spilled	water on my keyboard.

Use "when" to link the past continuous and past simple.

Formation guide Visual guides break down English grammar into its simplest parts, showing you how to recreate even complex formations.

Vocabulary Throughout the book, vocabulary modules list the most common and useful English words and phrases for business, with visual cues to help you remember them.

Write-on lines You are encouraged to write your own translations of English words to create your own reference pages.

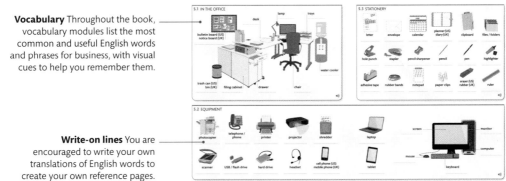

9

Practice modules

Each learning point is followed by carefully graded exercises that help to fix new language in your memory. Working through the exercises will help you remember what you have learned and become more fluent. Every exercise is introduced with a symbol to indicate which skill is being practiced.

 GRAMMAR
Apply new language rules in different contexts.

 READING
Examine target language in real-life English contexts.

LISTENING
Test your understanding of spoken English.

 VOCABULARY
Cement your understanding of key vocabulary.

 WRITING
Practice producing written passages of English text.

SPEAKING
Compare your spoken English to model audio recordings.

Module number Every module is identified with a unique number, so you can easily locate answers and related audio.

Exercise instruction Every exercise is introduced with a brief instruction, telling you what you need to do.

41.6 FILL IN THE GAPS USING THE WORDS IN THE PANEL

Do you have ___*enough*___ bread?

❶ I've eaten _____ many chocolates.

❷ How _____ glasses do we need?

❸ There's too _____ sauce on this.

❹ How _____ should we tip here?

much	much	many
	too	~~enough~~

Sample answer The first question of each exercise is answered for you, to help make the task easy to understand.

Space for writing You are encouraged to write your answers in the book for future reference.

Supporting graphics Visual cues are given to help you understand the exercises.

Speaking exercise This symbol indicates that you should say your answers out loud, then compare them to model recordings included in your audio files.

4.7 SAY THE SENTENCES OUT LOUD, USING SHORT FORMS

I am not very busy today.
> *I'm not very busy today.*

❶ These polo shirts are not made in Vietnam.

❷ This restaurant does not use British meat.

❸ The onions in this market are not local.

❹ I am not Brazilian, but I work in Brazil.

❺ The company does not have overseas clients.

Listening exercise This symbol indicates that you should listen to an audio track in order to answer the questions in the exercise.

20.6 LISTEN TO THE AUDIO, THEN NUMBER THE PICTURES IN THE ORDER THEY ARE DESCRIBED

 Ⓐ ☐

 Ⓑ ①

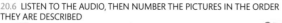 Ⓒ ☐

 Ⓓ ☐

 Ⓔ ☐

Supporting audio This symbol shows that the answers to the exercise are available as audio tracks. Listen to them after completing the exercise.

Audio

English for Everyone features extensive supporting audio materials. You are encouraged to use them as much as you can, to improve your understanding of spoken English, and to make your own accent and pronunciation more natural. Each file can be played, paused, and repeated as often as you like, until you are confident you understand what has been said.

LISTENING EXERCISES
This symbol indicates that you should listen to an audio track in order to answer the questions in the exercise.

SUPPORTING AUDIO
This symbol indicates that extra audio material is available for you to listen to after completing the module.

FREE AUDIO
website and app
www.dkefe.com

Track your progress

The course is designed to make it easy to monitor your progress, with regular summary and review modules. Answers are provided for every exercise, so you can see how well you have understood each teaching point.

Checklists Every unit ends with a checklist, where you can check off the new skills you have learned.

07 ✔ CHECKLIST
♂ Short answers ☐   **Aa** Contact information ☐   🔗 Exchanging contact details ☐

Review modules At the end of a group of units, you will find a more detailed review module, summarizing the language you have learned.

Check boxes Use these boxes to mark the skills you feel comfortable with. Go back and review anything you feel you need to practice further.

🔄 **REVIEW** THE ENGLISH YOU HAVE LEARNED IN UNITS 1–7

NEW LANGUAGE	SAMPLE SENTENCE	☑	UNIT
INTRODUCING YOURSELF AND OTHER PEOPLE	Good morning. My name's Alisha Sharma. This is my colleague, Edward.	☐	1.1, 1.5
PRESENT SIMPLE TO DESCRIBE ROUTINE WORK ACTIVITIES	We have a team meeting every Tuesday. The CEO works weekends if we're busy.	☐	2.1
COUNTRIES AND NATIONALITIES	These new mopeds are from Italy. I'm Brazilian, but I work in the US.	☐	4.1, 4.2, 4.3
NEGATIVE SENTENCES	I'm not French. I'm Canadian. The printer doesn't work!	☐	4.6
ASKING QUESTIONS	Do you have an appointment? Where is the staff room?	☐	6.1, 6.4, 6.8
EXCHANGING DETAILS, SHORT ANSWERS	Is this your email address? Yes, it is. Do you have a business card? No, I don't.	☐	7.1, 7.2, 7.7

29

29.2 ◀))
1 It's a special one for fire safety.
2 There's a nice café across the street.
3 We're meeting clients later this afternoon.
4 I have saved all the documents.

29.3 ◀))
1 Is your stapler broken? You **can** use mine.
2 She **doesn't have to** come to the training session. She did it last year.
3 You **have to** turn off the light if you're the last person to leave the office.
4 He **has to** test the fire alarm every Wednesday morning.
5 We **don't have to** wear a jacket and tie in the summer months.

29.4
1 Not given 2 False 3 True
4 True 5 False

29.8 ◀))
1 Could you **tell** Jan to call me back?
2 Could you **check** this report?
3 Would you mind **ordering** more pens?
4 Could you **mop** the floor, please?
5 Could you **come** to today's meeting?
6 Would you mind **calling** back later?
7 Would you mind **turning** the light off?
8 Could you **wash** these cups, please?
9 Could you **pass** around the reports?
10 Would you mind **booking** me a taxi?
11 Could you **show** our clients around?

29.9
1 False 2 False 3 True 4 True

29.10 ◀))
1. Could you book a meeting room?
2. Could you send Sam Davies an email?
3. Could you call our supplier?
4. Would you mind booking a meeting room?
5. Would you mind sending Sam Davies an email?
6. Would you mind calling our supplier?

Answers Find the answers to every exercise printed at the back of the book.

Exercise numbers Match these numbers to the unique identifier at the top-left corner of each exercise.

Audio This symbol indicates that the answers can also be listened to.

01 Meeting new colleagues

You can use formal or informal English to introduce yourself and greet colleagues or co-workers, depending on the situation and the people you are meeting.

⚙️ **New language** Alphabet and spelling
Aa Vocabulary Introductions and greetings
🧩 **New skill** Introducing yourself to co-workers

1.1 KEY LANGUAGE INTRODUCING YOURSELF

English uses a variety of polite phrases for introducing yourself and greeting your co-workers.

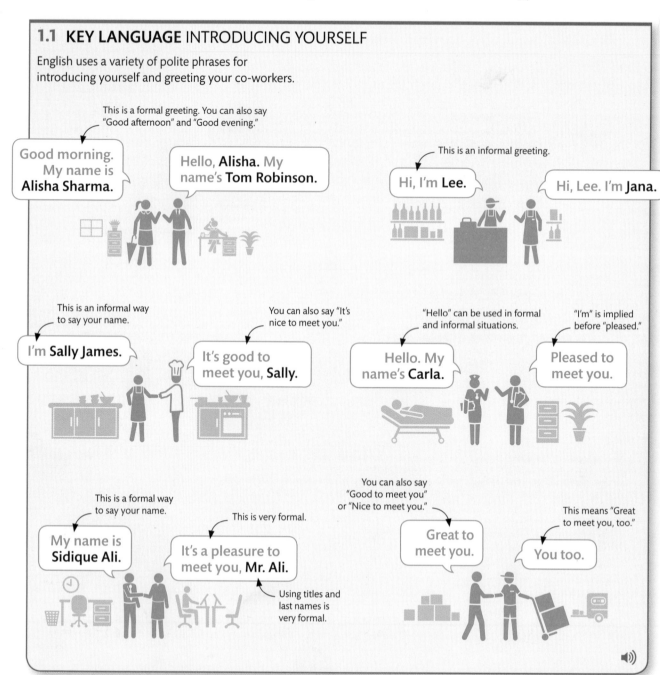

This is a formal greeting. You can also say "Good afternoon" and "Good evening."

Good morning. My name is **Alisha Sharma.**

Hello, **Alisha.** My name's **Tom Robinson.**

This is an informal greeting.

Hi, I'm **Lee.**

Hi, Lee. I'm **Jana.**

This is an informal way to say your name.

I'm **Sally James.**

You can also say "It's nice to meet you."

It's good to meet you, **Sally.**

"Hello" can be used in formal and informal situations.

Hello. My name's **Carla.**

"I'm" is implied before "pleased."

Pleased to meet you.

This is a formal way to say your name.

My name is **Sidique Ali.**

This is very formal.

It's a pleasure to meet you, **Mr. Ali.**

Using titles and last names is very formal.

You can also say "Good to meet you" or "Nice to meet you."

Great to meet you.

This means "Great to meet you, too."

You too.

1.2 FILL IN THE GAPS USING THE WORDS IN THE PANEL

It's good to _____meet_____ you.

1. Hello. My _name is_ Sebastian. ✓
2. Good _to meeting_. My name is Joe Carr. ✗
3. Hi, Marie. _This is_ Clive. ✓
4. It's great to meet you, _too_, Sven. ✓
5. It's a _pleasure_ to meet you. ✓

afternoon	pleasure	~~meet~~
I'm	name's	too

🔊

1.3 PRONUNCIATION THE ALPHABET

Listen to how the letters of the alphabet are pronounced in English when they are said individually.

Aa Bb Cc Dd Ee
Ff Gg Hh Ii Jj Kk
Ll Mm Nn Oo Pp
Qq Rr Ss Tt Uu
Vv Ww Xx Yy Zz

🔊

1.4 LISTEN TO THE AUDIO AND MARK THE NAMES YOU HEAR

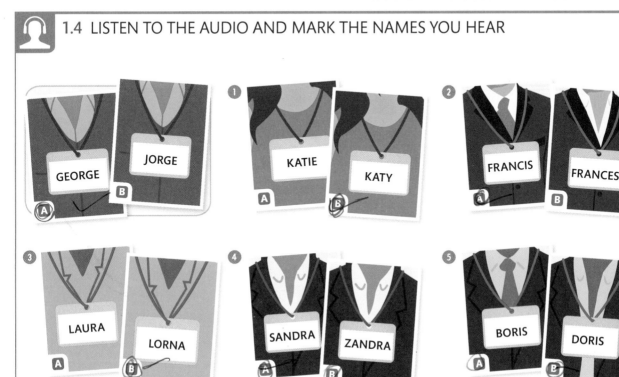

GEORGE (A) / JORGE (B)

1. KATIE (A) / KATY (B)

2. FRANCIS (A) / FRANCES (B)

3. LAURA (A) / LORNA (B)

4. SANDRA (A) / ZANDRA (B)

5. BORIS (A) / DORIS (B)

1.5 KEY LANGUAGE INTRODUCING OTHER PEOPLE

You can also use polite formal and informal phrases to introduce your co-workers to each other.

This is a formal introduction.

May I introduce **Maria Diaz? Maria is our sales manager for Europe.**

It's good to meet you, **Maria.**

It's a pleasure to meet you too.

This is an informal introduction.

Amit, meet Edward. **Edward, Amit and I work together.**

Great to meet you, **Edward.**

This is a formal introduction.

I'd like you to meet **Zoe Carr.**

It's nice to meet you, **Ms. Carr.**

Use "this is" to introduce other people in less formal situations.

This is **my new assistant, Levi.**

Hi, **Levi.** Good to meet you.

1.6 REWRITE THE SENTENCES, CORRECTING THE ERRORS

Hello, Sam. Nice meet you.
Hello, Sam. Nice to meet you.

❶ To meet you, it's a pleasure, too.
It's a pleasure to meet you

❷ Hi, I'm name's Adedeyo.
Hi, I'm names Adedeyo

❸ Greet to meet you.
Great to meet you

❹ This my new colleague, Martin.
This is my new colleague Martin

❺ Marisa, meeting Roula, my partner.
Marisa meeting Roula partner

❻ It's good to meet to you, Katherine.
It's good to meet to you Katherine

❼ I may introduce Claudia Gomez, our new CEO?
I may introduction Claudia Gomez our new CEO

1.7 LISTEN TO THE AUDIO AND ANSWER THE QUESTIONS

Jill has started a new job. She goes to a meeting with her new colleagues, Mr. Singh and Daniel.

What is Jill's role at the company?

Design assistant ☐
Finance manager ☑
Intern ☐

1 What is Jill's last name?
Greene ☑
Cheam ☐
Green ☐

2 How long has Mr. Singh been working with Spandone and Co.?
14 years ☑
15 years ☐
16 years ☐

3 What is Mr. Singh's role at Spandone and Co.?
Lawyer ☐
CEO ☐
Accountant ☑

4 Which two people are meeting for the first time?
Jill and Daniel ☑
Jill and Mr. Singh ☑
Daniel and Mr. Singh ☐

1.8 SAY THE SENTENCES OUT LOUD, FILLING IN THE GAPS USING THE WORDS IN THE PANEL

May I _introduce_ Marta Lopez? Marta and I _work_ together.

1 Hello, Mr. Lucas. It's a _pleasure_ to meet _you_ .

2 Ashley, _meet_ André. André and I work on the _same_ project.

3 _Hello_ , Sophie. My _name is_ Rachel Davies. Great to meet you.

4 _This_ is my colleague, Hayley. We went to college _together_ .

5 It's _good_ to meet you, Cori. _My_ name's Angel.

6 Hello, James. _It's_ really nice _to_ meet you. My name's Alex.

good	together	It's	My	to
~~introduce~~	name's	pleasure	Hello
meet	same	you	This	~~work~~

02 Everyday work activities

Use the present simple to talk about things that you do regularly, such as your daily tasks or everyday work routines.

⚙ **New language** Present simple
Aa Vocabulary Work activities
🧩 **New skill** Talking about workplace routines

2.1 KEY LANGUAGE THE PRESENT SIMPLE

Use the present simple to talk about things that happen regularly as part of a routine.

Every morning, we prepare the food and Justin sets the tables.

🔊

2.2 HOW TO FORM THE PRESENT SIMPLE

With regular verbs, use the base form of the verb to make the present simple with "I," "you," "we," and "they." With "he," "she," and "it," add "s" to the base form.

SUBJECT	VERB	REST OF SENTENCE
I / You / We / They	prepare	the food every morning.
He / She	prepares	

2.3 FURTHER EXAMPLES THE PRESENT SIMPLE

"Be" with "I" is "I am." The short form is "I'm."

I'm a lifeguard at the local pool.

Present simple form of "be" with "he," "she," and "it."

Mia is an excellent tour guide.

They have a meeting every morning.

We usually stop for tea and coffee at 11.

Present simple form of "be" with "we," "you," and "they."

Stephanie works from home on Mondays.

We are always busy in the evening.

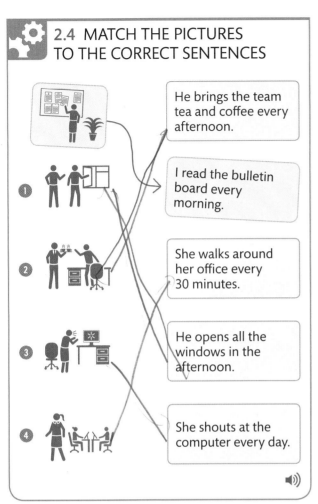

2.4 MATCH THE PICTURES TO THE CORRECT SENTENCES

He brings the team tea and coffee every afternoon.

I read the bulletin board every morning.

She walks around her office every 30 minutes.

He opens all the windows in the afternoon.

She shouts at the computer every day.

2.5 FILL IN THE GAPS USING THE WORDS IN THE PANEL

We __have__ a meeting every day.

1. She __is is is__ a hairdresser.

2. He __travel__ by train every morning.
   travels

3. She __leaves__ work at 6pm every day.

4. She __drinks__ coffee twice a day.

5. He __eats__ lunch at a local café.
   eats

| eats | is | drinks |
| leaves | ~~have~~ | travels |

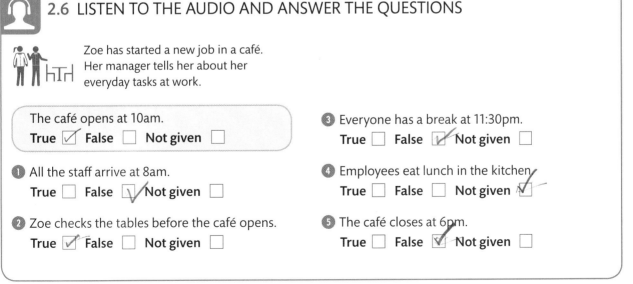

2.6 LISTEN TO THE AUDIO AND ANSWER THE QUESTIONS

Zoe has started a new job in a café. Her manager tells her about her everyday tasks at work.

The café opens at 10am.
True ☑ False ☐ Not given ☐

1. All the staff arrive at 8am.
   True ☐ False ☐ Not given ☑

2. Zoe checks the tables before the café opens.
   True ☑ False ☐ Not given ☐

3. Everyone has a break at 11:30pm.
   True ☐ False ☐ Not given ☑

4. Employees eat lunch in the kitchen.
   True ☐ False ☐ Not given ☑

5. The café closes at 6pm.
   True ☐ False ☐ Not given ☑

2.7 ⚠ COMMON MISTAKES THE PRESENT SIMPLE WITH "HE," "SHE," AND "IT"

It's easy to forget to add "s" to the base form of the verb in the present simple with third-person singular pronouns, "he," "she," and "it."

Add an "s" to the base form of the verb.

The CEO works on Sundays.

The CEO work on Sundays. ✖

This is wrong.

2.8 CROSS OUT THE INCORRECT WORD IN EACH SENTENCE

 She ~~make~~ / **makes** tea and coffee before the team meeting every Friday.

1. The head of marketing **speak** / ~~speaks~~ for about an hour at every team meeting.

2. Arianna and Gabriel **read** / ~~reads~~ their emails first thing every morning.

3. The photocopier ~~stop~~ / **stops** working if we don't load the paper carefully.

4. The owners of the hotel **visit** / ~~visits~~ it at the end of every month.

5. The cleaner **start** / ~~starts~~ work at 6am every day. The office is always clean in the mornings.

🔊

2.9 USE THE CHART TO CREATE EIGHT CORRECT SENTENCES AND SAY THEM OUT LOUD

I work from Monday to Friday.

| I / You / She / My manager | work / works / have / has | from Monday to Friday. / a meeting every morning. |

🔊

OUR TEAM

Meet the manager

Our Head of Customer Services describes a typical working day

Sumiko Akimoto, our Head of Customer Services, describes a typical day at work. "Every morning, even in the winter, I ride my bicycle to work. I arrive at work early and then walk through the departments to talk to the staff. It is important for me to know what is happening in the company so that I can share any useful information with clients. Next, I read my emails and use them to help me write a list of things to do during the day. I rarely do everything on the list, but it's useful to help me plan my day.

During my morning coffee break, I talk to my team members about my list and sometimes delegate tasks to them. At lunchtime, many of my colleagues go to a local Italian restaurant to eat, but I stay in the office and eat a packed lunch. I like to deal with all my emails by 5 o'clock. Sometimes I can leave work at 5:30, but I usually leave at 6 o'clock. To help me relax after work, I turn off my phone as soon as I get home."

Sumiko cycles to work every day.	True ☑	False ☐
❶ She reads her emails first thing every morning.	True ☐	False ☑
❷ She writes a list of things to do that day.	True ☑	False ☐
❸ She meets her colleagues to talk about the day's work.	True ☑	False ☒
❹ Sumiko goes to a local restaurant for lunch every day.	True ☐	False ☑
❺ She tries to deal with all her emails by 5 o'clock.	True ☑	False ☐
❻ Sumiko always leaves work at 6 o'clock.	True ☑	False ☑
❼ She turns her phone off when she gets home.	True ☑	False ☐

02 ✓ CHECKLIST

⚙ Present simple ☐   **Aa** Work activities ☐   👥 Talking about workplace routines ☐

3.1 COUNTRIES

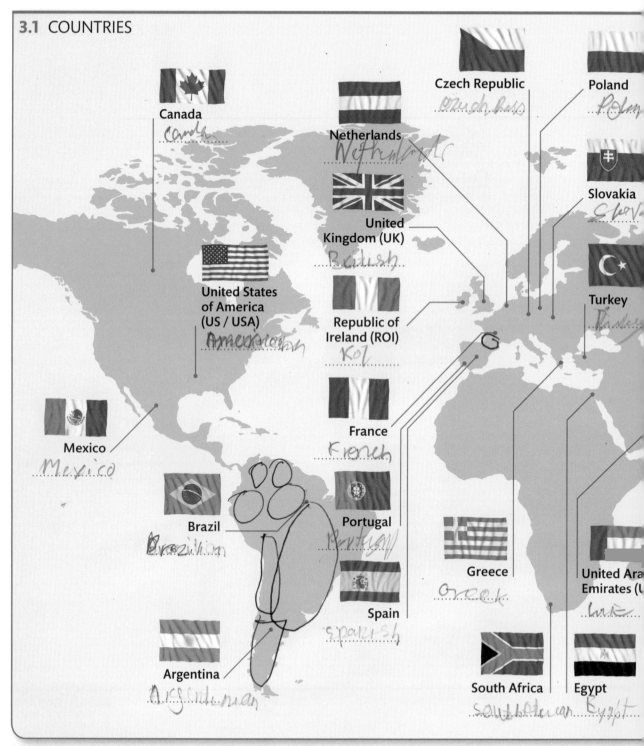

Canada
canda

Czech Republic
czech Res

Poland
Polen

Netherlands
Netherlands

Slovakia
Slov

United
Kingdom (UK)
British

Turkey
Tirkey

United States
of America
(US / USA)
American

Republic of
Ireland (ROI)
ROI

Mexico
Mexico

France
French

Brazil
Brazilian

Portugal
Portugall

Greece
Greek

United Arab
Emirates (U...
UAE

Spain
Spanish

Argentina
Argentinian

South Africa
South African

Egypt
Egypt

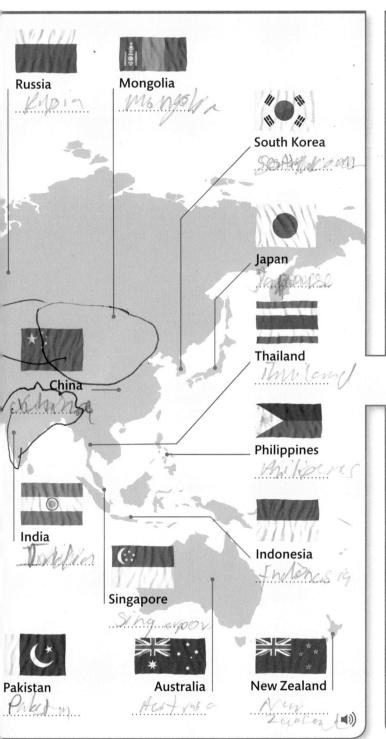

Russia

Rusia

Mongolia

mongolia

South Korea

South Korea

Japan

Japanese

Thailand

Thailand

Philippines

Philipines

China

china

India

India

Indonesia

Indonesia

Singapore

Singapoor

Pakistan

Pakistan

Australia

Australia

New Zealand

New Zealand ◀))

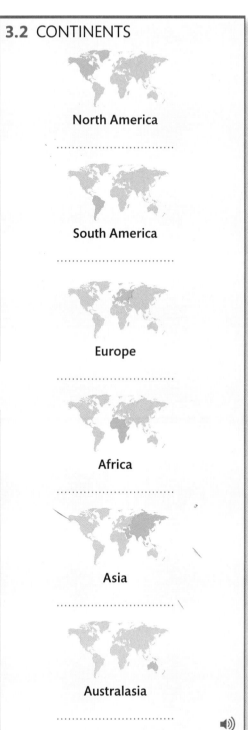

North America

....

South America

....

Europe

....

Africa

....

Asia

....

Australasia

....

◀))

04 Business around the world

English uses "from" or nationality adjectives to talk about where products or people come from. "From" can also refer to your company or department.

⚙ **New language** Negative statements
Aa Vocabulary Countries and nationalities
🧩 **New skill** Saying where things are from

4.1 VOCABULARY NATIONALITY ADJECTIVES

Nationality adjectives are based on country names. Most end in "-ese," "-an," "-ish," "-ean," or "-ian," but some are irregular.

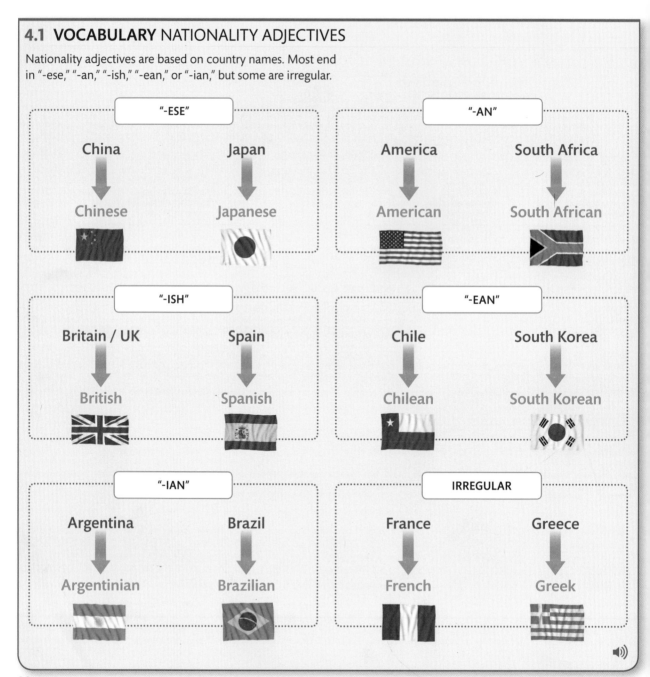

"-ESE"

China → Chinese

Japan → Japanese

"-AN"

America → American

South Africa → South African

"-ISH"

Britain / UK → British

Spain → Spanish

"-EAN"

Chile → Chilean

South Korea → South Korean

"-IAN"

Argentina → Argentinian

Brazil → Brazilian

IRREGULAR

France → French

Greece → Greek

4.2 KEY LANGUAGE COUNTRIES AND NATIONALITIES

To talk about where products were made or what country people come from, use "from" with a country name, or a nationality adjective.

"FROM" + COUNTRY

These new mopeds are from Italy.

NATIONALITY ADJECTIVE

These new mopeds are Italian.

4.3 FURTHER EXAMPLES COUNTRIES AND NATIONALITIES

These smartphones are from Japan.

The new CEO is from Switzerland.

These Indian dresses are excellent value.

I'm Russian, but I regularly visit the US.

4.4 CROSS OUT THE INCORRECT WORD IN EACH SENTENCE

These monitors are from China / ~~Chinese~~.

1. I'm on the ~~Europe~~ / European sales team.

2. Our ~~Chile~~ / Chilean office is in Santiago.

3. We sell leather shoes from Spain / ~~Spanish~~.

4. My job is to watch the ~~Asia~~ / Asian markets.

5. Book a trip to Mexico / ~~Mexican~~ with us.

4.5 LISTEN TO THE AUDIO AND MATCH THE PRODUCTS TO THE PLACE NAMES

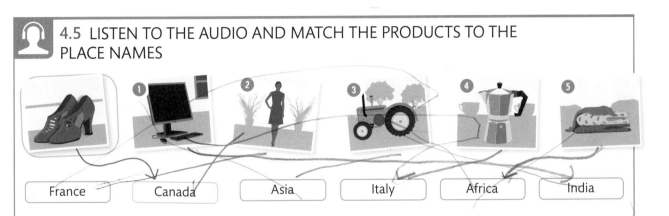

France | Canada | Asia | Italy | Africa | India

4.6 KEY LANGUAGE CONTRACTED NEGATIVES

Adding "not" makes a positive statement negative.
"Not" is often used in its contracted form.

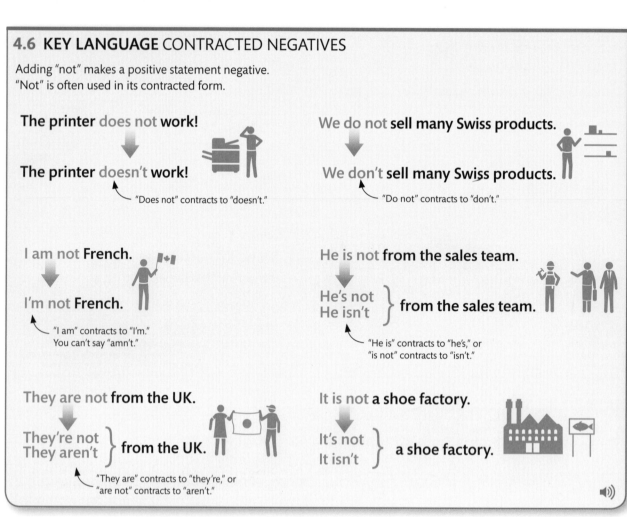

The printer does not **work!**

The printer doesn't **work!**

"Does not" contracts to "doesn't."

We do not sell many Swiss products.

We don't sell many Swiss products.

"Do not" contracts to "don't."

I am not French.

I'm not French.

"I am" contracts to "I'm."
You can't say "amn't."

He is not from the sales team.

He's not
He isn't } **from the sales team.**

"He is" contracts to "he's," or
"is not" contracts to "isn't."

They are not from the UK.

They're not
They aren't } **from the UK.**

"They are" contracts to "they're," or
"are not" contracts to "aren't."

It is not a shoe factory.

It's not
It isn't } **a shoe factory.**

4.7 SAY THE SENTENCES OUT LOUD, USING SHORT FORMS

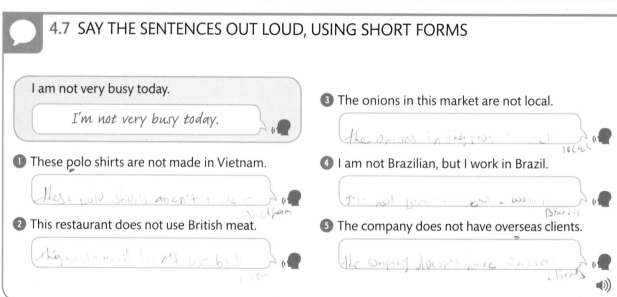

I am not very busy today.

I'm not very busy today.

1 These polo shirts are not made in Vietnam.

These polo shirts aren't made in Vietnam

2 This restaurant does not use British meat.

this restaurant doesn't use beef

3 The onions in this market are not local.

the onions in this market aren't local

4 I am not Brazilian, but I work in Brazil.

I'm not brazilian but I work in Brazil

5 The company does not have overseas clients.

the company doesn't have overseas clients

4.8 KEY LANGUAGE SAYING WHERE YOU WORK

"From" can also refer to a company or department.

> I'm George. I'm from the marketing department in New York.

> And this is Barbara. She's from QuickStyle Printers.

> I'm Nisha. I'm from finance.

People often leave out "the" and "department" when they say what department they are from.

4.9 READ THE COMPANY PROFILE AND ANSWER THE QUESTIONS

Guitar City is a new company.
True ☐ **False** ☑

1 Giorgio Michalis is from Greece.
True ☒ **False** ☑

2 Giorgio has one Guitar City guitar.
True ☐ **False** ☑

3 Pete Donnelly works in production.
True ☑ **False** ☐

4 The guitars are made of wood from rainforests.
True ☐ **False** ☑

5 Each guitar has a beautiful wood pattern.
True ☐ **False** ☑

6 Some of the artists are Polish.
True ☑ **False** ☐

Guitar City

HOME | PRODUCTS | ABOUT | CONTACT

About us

Established in 1965, Guitar City makes guitars for some of the most famous musicians in the world. The award-winning Greek guitarist Giorgio Michalis always uses our guitars and believes that they are the best that he has ever played. "The sound of all my Guitar City guitars is amazing," he says.

Our guitars are mostly made from recycled aluminum and are much lighter than the usual, wooden ones. Pete Donnelly from our production department also says that these guitars are better for the environment. "We do not use any wooden materials from rainforests and we make all the main guitar body parts from recycled materials."

Guitar City guitars also look really great. They do not have the natural beauty of wood, but each guitar is hand painted by a top artist from our creative design team. With artists from Kenya, Poland, Mexico, and Laos, we have designs to suit everyone.

---

04 ✔ CHECKLIST

⚙ Negative statements ☐   **Aa** Countries and nationalities ☐   🧩 Saying where things are from ☐

5.1 IN THE OFFICE

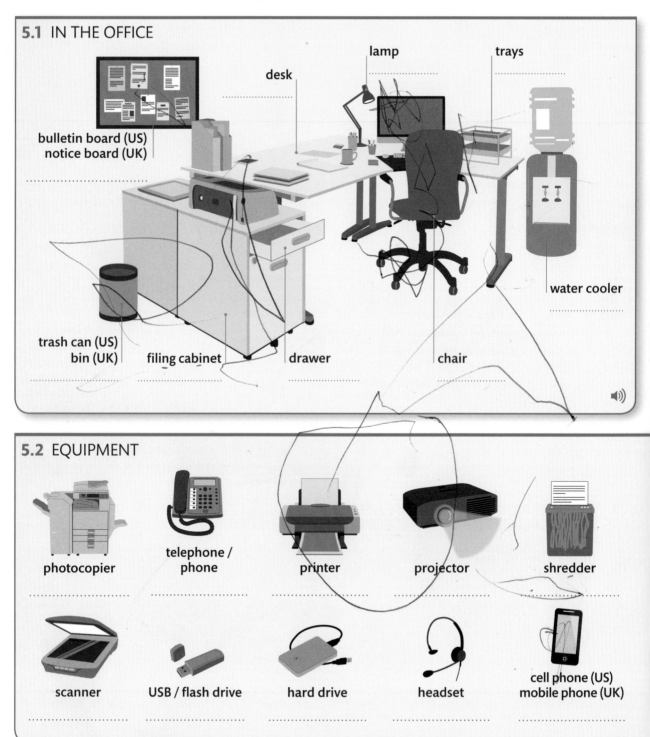

bulletin board (US)
notice board (UK)

desk

lamp

trays

trash can (US)
bin (UK)

filing cabinet

drawer

chair

water cooler

5.2 EQUIPMENT

photocopier

telephone /
phone

printer

projector

shredder

scanner

USB / flash drive

hard drive

headset

cell phone (US)
mobile phone (UK)

5.3 STATIONERY

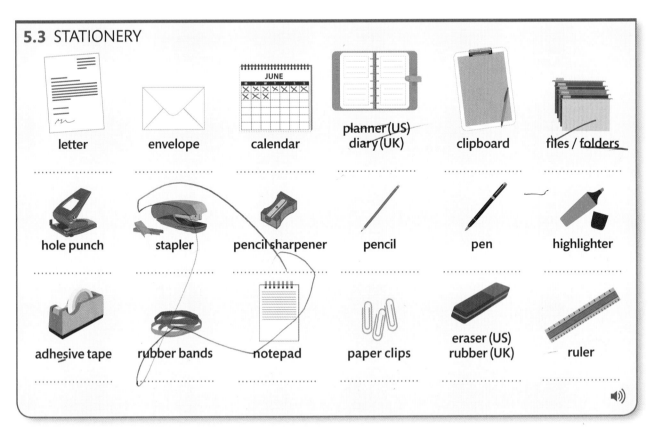

letter

envelope

calendar

planner (US)
diary (UK)

clipboard

files / folders

hole punch

stapler

pencil sharpener

pencil

pen

highlighter

adhesive tape

rubber bands

notepad

paper clips

eraser (US)
rubber (UK)

ruler

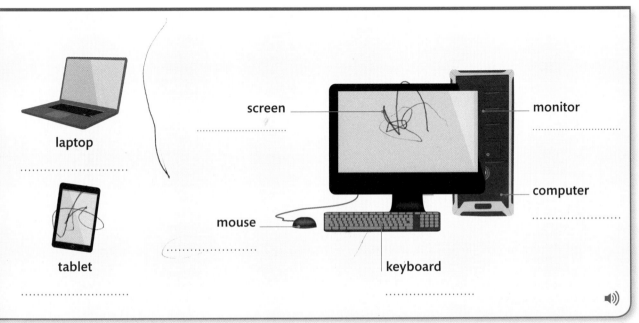

laptop

tablet

screen

monitor

mouse

keyboard

computer

06 Asking questions at work

It is important to use the correct word order and question words in English questions, depending on whether the questions are open-ended.

⚙ **New language** Forming questions
Aa Vocabulary Office equipment
🧩 **New skill** Asking colleagues questions

6.1 KEY LANGUAGE SIMPLE QUESTIONS WITH "TO BE"

Is this **where I can pay?**

No. Our machines are broken.

Are the meeting rooms all busy?

Yes. I'm afraid so

6.2 HOW TO FORM SIMPLE QUESTIONS WITH "TO BE"

In a statement, the subject comes before the verb. In a question, the subject and verb swap places.

This is where I can pay.

Is this where I can pay?

Verb ⬆ ⬆ Subject

6.3 REWRITE THE QUESTIONS, PUTTING THE WORDS IN THE CORRECT ORDER

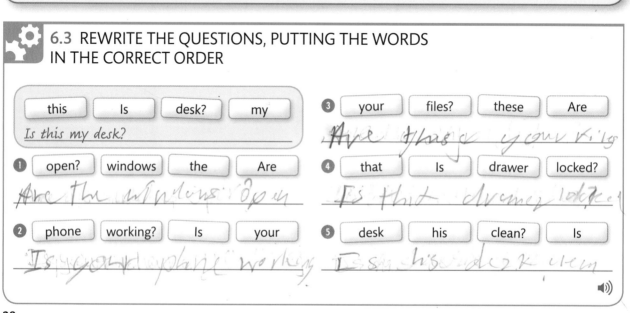

| this | Is | desk? | my |

Is this my desk?

❶ | open? | windows | the | Are |

Are the windows open

❷ | phone | working? | Is | your |

Is your phone working

❸ | your | files? | these | Are |

Are these your files

❹ | that | Is | drawer | locked? |

Is that drawer locked

❺ | desk | his | clean? | Is |

Is his desk clean

28

6.4 KEY LANGUAGE SIMPLE QUESTIONS WITH "DO"

To form questions in sentences without the verb
"to be," start the question with "do" or "does."

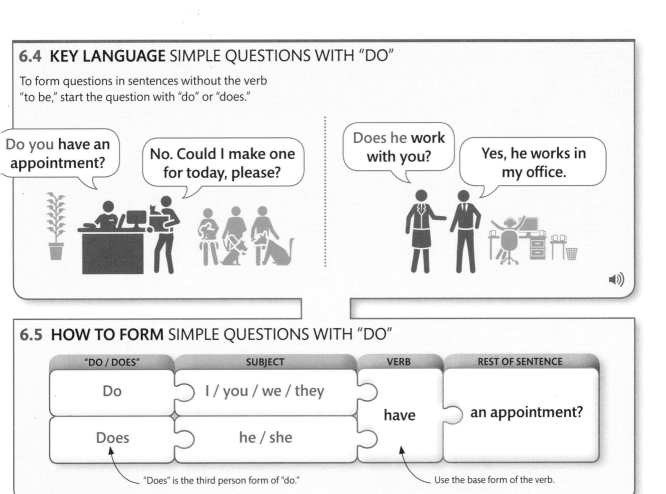

Do you **have an appointment?**

No. Could I make one for today, please?

Does he work with you?

Yes, he works in my office.

6.5 HOW TO FORM SIMPLE QUESTIONS WITH "DO"

"DO / DOES"	SUBJECT	VERB	REST OF SENTENCE
Do	I / you / we / they	have	an appointment?
Does	he / she		

"Does" is the third person form of "do."

Use the base form of the verb.

6.6 FILL IN THE GAPS USING "DO" OR "DOES"

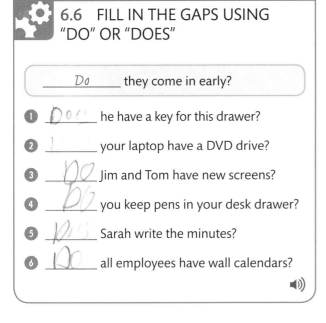

_____Do_____ they come in early?

1. ____Does____ he have a key for this drawer?
2. ____Does____ your laptop have a DVD drive?
3. ____Do____ Jim and Tom have new screens?
4. ____Do____ you keep pens in your desk drawer?
5. ____Does____ Sarah write the minutes?
6. ____Do____ all employees have wall calendars?

6.7 LISTEN TO THE AUDIO AND NUMBER THE QUESTIONS IN THE ORDER YOU HEAR THEM

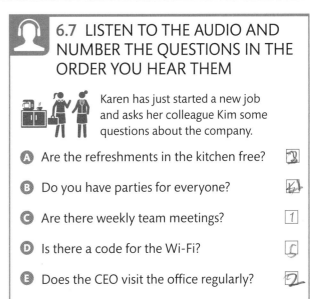

Karen has just started a new job and asks her colleague Kim some questions about the company.

- **A** Are the refreshments in the kitchen free? [3]
- **B** Do you have parties for everyone? [4]
- **C** Are there weekly team meetings? [1]
- **D** Is there a code for the Wi-Fi? [5]
- **E** Does the CEO visit the office regularly? [2]

6.8 KEY LANGUAGE ASKING OPEN QUESTIONS

Use question words such as "when," "where," "how," or "why"
to ask questions that can't be answered with "yes" or "no."

Where is the staff room?

Go down to the second floor.

When does Mia start work?

She usually starts at nine.

6.9 FURTHER EXAMPLES OPEN QUESTIONS

The auxilary "do / does" comes before the subject.

How does the scanner work?

What would you like to drink?

Invert the subject and the verb to form open questions with "to be."

Where is the cafeteria?

Why is he late?

The main verb comes at the end in questions without "to be."

Who is giving the presentation?

When does the meeting start?

6.10 CROSS OUT THE INCORRECT WORD IN EACH QUESTION

When / ~~What~~ are you going on vacation?

1. Where / How are the cups?

2. Who / What is the photocopier code?

3. Why / How do I turn off the screen?

4. Why / Who is this drawer always locked?

5. Where / When does the cafeteria open?

6. Why / Who do I ask for printer ink?

7. What / When do you discuss at meetings?

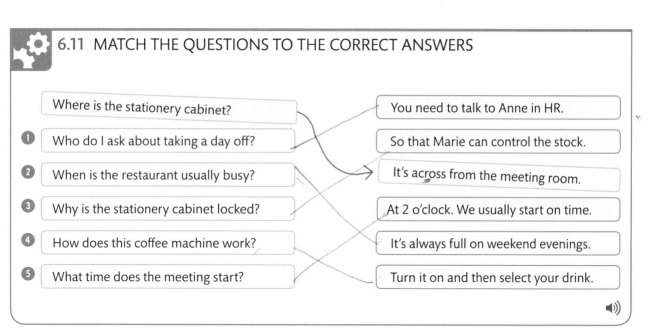

6.11 MATCH THE QUESTIONS TO THE CORRECT ANSWERS

Where is the stationery cabinet?

1. Who do I ask about taking a day off?
2. When is the restaurant usually busy?
3. Why is the stationery cabinet locked?
4. How does this coffee machine work?
5. What time does the meeting start?

You need to talk to Anne in HR.

So that Marie can control the stock.

It's across from the meeting room.

At 2 o'clock. We usually start on time.

It's always full on weekend evenings.

Turn it on and then select your drink.

6.12 MARK THE QUESTIONS THAT ARE CORRECT

Who is in your team? ☑
What is in your team? ☐

1. What I can do to help you? ☐
   What can I do to help you? ☑

2. Do you know where the key is? ☑
   Does you know where the key is? ☐

3. When does the store open? ☑
   When do the store open? ☐

4. Who do I connect the keyboard? ☐
   How do I connect the keyboard? ☑

5. Why is her desk always a mess? ☑
   Why does her desk always a mess? ☐

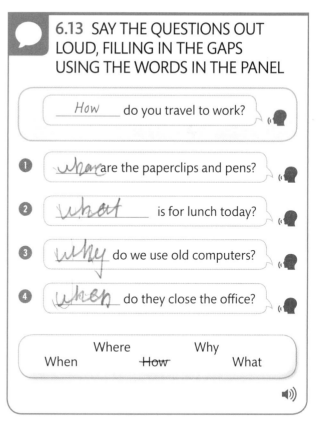

6.13 SAY THE QUESTIONS OUT LOUD, FILLING IN THE GAPS USING THE WORDS IN THE PANEL

How do you travel to work?

1. _Where_ are the paperclips and pens?
2. _what_ is for lunch today?
3. _why_ do we use old computers?
4. _when_ do they close the office?

When   Where   Why
      How   What

---

06 ✓ CHECKLIST

⚙ Forming questions ☐   **Aa** Office equipment ☐   🧩 Asking colleagues questions ☐

Exchanging details

When making new business contacts, there are
several phrases you can use to ask for their
details and offer yours in return.

⚙ **New language** Short answers
Aa Vocabulary Contact information
🧩 **New skill** Exchanging contact details

7.1 KEY LANGUAGE EXCHANGING CONTACT DETAILS

It is useful to know how to ask
for contact information from
a client or co-worker. Certain
stock phrases can be adapted
to many different situations.

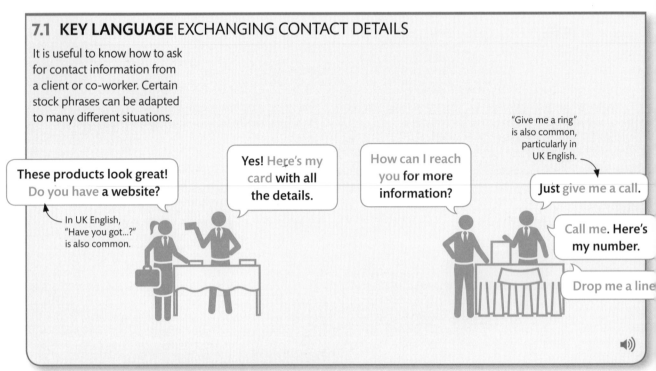

These products look great!
Do you have a website?

In UK English,
"Have you got...?"
is also common.

Yes! Here's my
card **with all**
the details.

How can I reach
you for more
information?

"Give me a ring"
is also common,
particularly in
UK English.

Just give me a call.

Call me. Here's
my number.

Drop me a line

7.2 VOCABULARY BUSINESS CARDS

name

Daniel Thompson

23 Long Lane
Redchester
RC3 7AP
United Kingdom

BIG films

Director

☎ 019230 8934   ✉ d.thompson@bigfilms.com

www.bigfilms.com

job title

Director

company name

Big Films

address

23 Long Lane Redchester
RC3 7AP United Kingdom

phone number

01.9230.8934

website

www.bigfilms.com

email address

d.thompson@bigfilms.com

7.3 PRONUNCIATION EMAIL ADDRESSES

There are set conventions for how to pronounce email address symbols such as "@" and "." in English.

(at) (hyphen) (underscore) (dot)

sue@super-cleaning_team.com

This is pronounced as one word, but domains like **.co.jp** and **.co.uk** are pronounced with initials: "dot co dot yoo kay"

🔊

 ## 7.4 LISTEN TO THE AUDIO, THEN NUMBER THE EMAIL ADDRESSES IN THE ORDER YOU HEAR THEM

 Six people are giving their contact details to someone they have met.

- **A** c.j.jones@global-exec.com — 2
- **B** joe@worldmail.co.jp — 5
- **C** c.jones@global-exec.com — 3
- **D** jay.jones@globalmail.com — 1
- **E** globalmail@jonesbrothers.com — 4
- **F** c.j.jones@global-exec.co.fr — 6

 ## 7.5 CROSS OUT THE INCORRECT WORD IN EACH SENTENCE

> Just ~~make~~ / give me a call when you're ready.

1. Do you ~~do~~ / have a website I can look up?
2. Your job title / ~~name~~ isn't listed here.
3. Just ~~fall~~ / drop me a line for more details.
4. How can I reach / ~~touch~~ you to follow up?
5. Is this your phone number / ~~address~~?
6. Here's my contact / ~~business~~ card.
7. ~~Say~~ / Call me to arrange a meeting.
8. Drop me a line / ~~word~~ to follow up next week.

🔊

 ## 7.6 LOOK AT THE BUSINESS CARDS AND ANSWER THE QUESTIONS

> McKay & Sons is a travel agent. **True** ☐ **False** ☑

1. McKay and Sons has a website. **True** ☑ **False** ☐
2. Steven McKay is a Web Designer. **True** ☐ **False** ☑
3. Nancy Li has a website. **True** ☑ **False** ☐
4. City Zoo is on Madison Avenue. **True** ☐ **False** ☑
5. Nancy works in Human Resources. **True** ☐ **False** ☑
6. Nancy has an email address. **True** ☑ **False** ☐

McKay & Sons
Architects
www.mckayandsons.com

Steven McKay
Managing Director

📞 1200 400 589
✉ s.mckay@mckayandsons.net

City Zoo
2045 Mason Avenue, Madison, WI 54229

Nancy Li
Assistant Zoologist
(608) 233-4487
nancyli@cityzoo.org

7.7 KEY LANGUAGE SHORT ANSWERS

You will often hear short answers such as "Yes, I am" in English-speaking workplaces. It is more polite to use a short answer than to just answer "Yes" or "No."

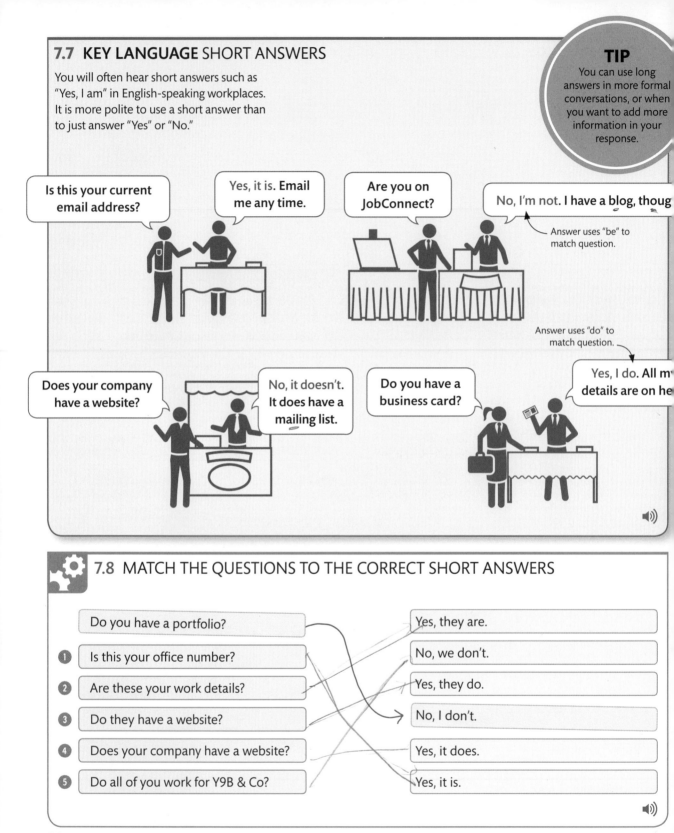

Is this your current email address?

Yes, it is. **Email me any time.**

Are you on JobConnect?

No, I'm not. **I have a blog, thoug**

Answer uses "be" to match question.

Answer uses "do" to match question.

Does your company have a website?

No, it doesn't. **It does have a mailing list.**

Do you have a business card?

Yes, I do. **All m details are on he**

7.8 MATCH THE QUESTIONS TO THE CORRECT SHORT ANSWERS

Do you have a portfolio?

Yes, they are.

1 Is this your office number?

No, we don't.

2 Are these your work details?

Yes, they do.

3 Do they have a website?

No, I don't.

4 Does your company have a website?

Yes, it does.

5 Do all of you work for Y9B & Co?

Yes, it is.

7.9 RESPOND OUT LOUD TO THE AUDIO, FILLING IN THE GAPS

Do I have your phone number?

Yes, _you do_ .

④ Does your website have a contact form?

No, _I don't_ .

① Is that your company's address?

No, _I don't_ .

⑤ Do they have a brochure?

Yes, _I do_ .

② Are these details still correct?

Yes, _they are_.

⑥ Do you want to arrange a meeting?

Yes, _I do_ .

③ Do you have a website?

Yes, _I do_ .

⑦ Do you have an office in the city?

No, _I don't_ .

🔊

---

07 ✓ CHECKLIST

⚙ Short answers ☐   **Aa** Contact information ☐   Exchanging contact details ☐

♺ REVIEW THE ENGLISH YOU HAVE LEARNED IN UNITS 1–7

NEW LANGUAGE	SAMPLE SENTENCE	☑	UNIT
INTRODUCING YOURSELF AND OTHER PEOPLE	Good morning. My name's Alisha Sharma. This is my colleague, Edward.	☐	1.1, 1.5
PRESENT SIMPLE TO DESCRIBE ROUTINE WORK ACTIVITIES	We have a team meeting every Tuesday. The CEO works weekends if we're busy.	☐	2.1
COUNTRIES AND NATIONALITIES	These new mopeds are from Italy. I'm Brazilian, but I work in the US.	☐	4.1, 4.2, 4.3
NEGATIVE SENTENCES	I'm not French. I'm Canadian. The printer doesn't work!	☐	4.6
ASKING QUESTIONS	Do you have an appointment? Where is the staff room?	☐	6.1, 6.4, 6.8
EXCHANGING DETAILS, SHORT ANSWERS	Is this your email address? Yes, it is. Do you have a business card? No, I don't.	☐	7.1, 7.2, 7.7

08 Skills and experience

English uses the verb "have" to talk about people's skills, experience, and professional attributes. You might also hear "have got" in informal UK English.

⚙ **New language** "Have," "have got," articles
Aa **Vocabulary** Jobs and skills
🧩 **New skill** Writing a business profile

8.1 KEY LANGUAGE "HAVE"

Use "have" with nouns to talk about people's qualities or experience.

"Have" is an irregular verb. The third-person form is "has."

I have **good computer skills.**

My assistant has **an excellent phone manner.**

8.2 FURTHER EXAMPLES "HAVE" AND "HAVE GOT"

He has **excellent negotiation skills.**

They don't have **good people skills.**

In negatives, "do not" or its short form "don't" sits before "have."

"Have got" is used in informal spoken UK English.

Have you got **any catering experience?**

She's got **a positive attitude.**

This short form of "has got" is informal.

8.3 HOW TO FORM STATEMENTS USING "HAVE"

SUBJECT	"HAVE" / "HAS"	REST OF SENTENCE
I / You / We / They	have	good computer skills.
He / She	has	

With "he," "she," and "it," use "has."

8.4 CROSS OUT THE INCORRECT WORDS IN EACH SENTENCE

He ~~have~~ / has excellent typing skills.

1 They don't / ~~doesn't~~ have interviews today.

2 He ~~haven't~~ / hasn't got a diploma.

3 I don't have / ~~don't got~~ any experience.

4 Do you ~~has~~ / have good IT skills?

5 We ~~haves~~ / have monthly training sessions.

6 He ~~don't~~ / doesn't have experience with animals.

7 He's ~~have~~ / has a Master's degree.

8 They have / ~~got~~ a lot of inexperienced staff.

9 She's got / ~~have~~ super negotiation skills.

8.5 READ THE ONLINE PROFILE AND MARK THE STATEMENTS THAT ARE CORRECT

Sam Bradley · photographer

HOME | SKILLS | CONTACT

Experience:
I have a lot of experience in digital photography and photo editing. I love working with animals and nature, and I won my first regional competition when I was 13. In college, I chaired the Photography Club and arranged speakers, training, and field trips. I have some experience of working in an office, having spent a summer working for a nature magazine.

Skills:
- I have excellent photography and editing skills learned from my degree and many years of experience.
- I enjoy working in teams, on my own, and with animals.

Qualifications:
- **BA Dance and Drama** (2014)
- **Diploma in Pet Photography** (2016)

Sam has never edited photographs. ☐
Sam has edited photographs. ☑

1 Sam loves working with children. ☐
Sam loves working with animals. ☑

2 Sam won a regional competition. ☑
Sam won a national competition. ☐

3 Sam didn't organize field trips. ☐
Sam organized field trips at college. ☑

4 Sam worked in an office. ☑
Sam didn't work in an office. ☐

5 Sam has excellent photography skills. ☑
Sam has good negotiation skills. ☐

6 Sam's degree is is photography. ☑
Sam's degree is in dance and drama. ☐

7 Sam has a photography diploma. ☑
Sam has never studied photography. ☐

8.6 KEY LANGUAGE "A / AN / THE"

Use "a" or "an" to talk about jobs and workplaces if you are mentioning them for the first time. Use "the" to talk about something specific, or something you have mentioned before.

Use "a" because you are mentioning the restaurant for the first time.

I'm a waiter. I work in a popular restaurant. The restaurant is always busy.

Use "the" because you have already mentioned the restaurant.

8.7 FURTHER EXAMPLES "A / AN / THE"

Use "an" before a vowel sound.

I'm an intern at an advertising agency.

Isaac is a good hairdresser.

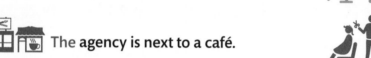

The agency is next to a café.

The hairdresser who works weekends is terrible.

8.8 FILL IN THE GAPS USING "A," "AN," OR "THE"

He works in _____a_____ hotel.

1. Oh, yes. I know _____the_____ hotel you mean.
2. Susan has _____a_____ diploma.
3. Is _____the_____ meeting on the second floor?
4. I work for _____a_____ large recruitment agency.
5. There's _____an_____ ad for a chef here.
6. I hired _____a_____ PA to help me out.
7. He works at _____the_____ hospital down the road.
8. Is there _____an_____ office in Mexico?

8.9 LISTEN TO THE AUDIO, THEN NUMBER THE PEOPLE IN THE ORDER THEY ARE DESCRIBED

A

B 1

C 5

D 3

E 4

F

8.10 KEY LANGUAGE THE ZERO ARTICLE

When English leaves out "a," "an," or "the" before a noun, this is called the zero article. Use the zero article with plurals when you are talking about things in general.

Refers to interviews in general, not specific interviews.

I get very nervous before interviews.

We're looking for people who can sell our products.

Refers to people in general, not specific individuals.

8.11 MARK THE SENTENCES THAT ARE CORRECT

Online profiles are really useful. ☑
The online profiles are really useful. ☐

1. He was out of the office today. ☑
   He was out of an office today. ☐

2. I have the excellent people skills. ☐
   I have excellent people skills. ☑

3. What skills do you need for this job? ☑
   What a skills do you need for this job? ☐

4. Have you read the job requirements? ☑
   Have you read a job requirements? ☐

5. She's a architect for a top company. ☐
   She's an architect for a top company. ☑

6. The new designer is very good. ☑
   A new designer is very good. ☐

8.12 READ THE COVER LETTER AND CROSS OUT THE INCORRECT WORDS

Dear Mr. Baxter,

I am writing to apply for the / a role of Library Assistant, which I saw advertised on your website. I have / got two years' experience working as a part-time assistant in my local library. The / A job involves working with a / the team of people and the public, so I have good people skills / the good people skills.

I do not have / have not a degree in Library and Information Studies, as an / the ad requested, but I have / has a degree in English Literature.

I look forward to hearing from you.
Yours sincerely,

Judy Stein

Judy Stein

---

08 ✓ CHECKLIST

⚙ "Have," "have got," articles ☐   **Aa** Jobs and skills ☐   🧩 Writing a business profile ☐

9.1 JOBS

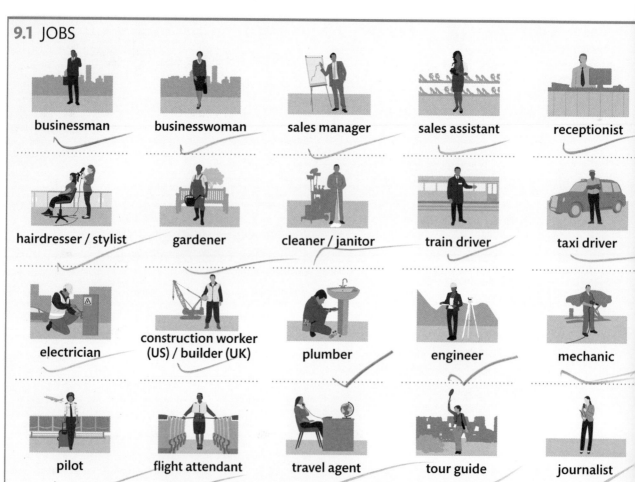

businessman	businesswoman	sales manager	sales assistant	receptionist
hairdresser / stylist	gardener	cleaner / janitor	train driver	taxi driver
electrician	construction worker (US) / builder (UK)	plumber	engineer	mechanic
pilot	flight attendant	travel agent	tour guide	journalist

9.2 EMPLOYMENT

full-time (F/T)
[a complete working week]

part-time (P/T)
[an incomplete working week]

permanent
[a long-term, salaried position]

temporary
[a short-term position with a known end date]

shift
[a period of work with a set number of hours]

waiter

waitress

chef

personal assistant / PA

scientist

librarian

teacher

judge

police officer

firefighter

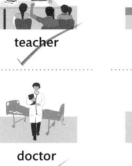

surgeon

doctor

nurse

dentist

vet

writer

designer

photographer

artist

musician

manager
[the person responsible or directing employees]

co-worker / colleague
[a person you work with in a profession]

assistant
[someone who does routine tasks for a senior person]

intern
[a person who works to gain experience]

apprentice
[a person who is learning a trade]

10 Choosing a job

Verbs such as "like," "enjoy," and "hate" express feelings about things. They are often used to talk about what activities people would like to do in a job.

⚙ **New language** "Like," "enjoy," and "hate"

Aa Vocabulary Workplace activities

🧩 **New skill** Finding the right job

10.1 KEY LANGUAGE LIKES AND DISLIKES

Use verbs such as "like," "enjoy," and "hate" to give your opinion on workplace activities. These can be followed by a noun, or by a gerund ("-ing" form of the verb) and a noun.

So, what kind of job are you looking for?

Verb ⟶   Noun

I don't want to work in IT. I hate computers.

I want to be a sales manager. I like giving presentations.

Verb   Gerund   Noun

10.2 FURTHER EXAMPLES LIKES AND DISLIKES

 I enjoy business trips.

 She hates writing contracts.

 He doesn't like interviews.

 I like meeting clients.

10.3 HOW TO FORM LIKES AND DISLIKES

Use a verb followed by a noun to give your opinion on a thing.

SUBJECT	VERB	NOUN
I	like / enjoy / don't like / hate	business trips.

Use a verb followed by a gerund and a noun to give your opinion on an activity.

SUBJECT	VERB	GERUND	NOUN
I	like / enjoy / don't like / hate	giving	presentations

Add "-ing" to the verb to form the gerund.

10.4 CROSS OUT THE INCORRECT WORDS IN EACH SENTENCE

Do you enjoy ~~meet~~ / meeting clients?

1 She ~~don't like~~ / doesn't like ~~like~~ using computers.

2 He likes training / ~~train~~ new colleagues.

3 I ~~hates~~ / hate long meetings.

4 We don't like / ~~doesn't like~~ lazy employees.

5 She enjoys ~~work~~ / working in a team.

10.5 LISTEN TO THE AUDIO AND MARK WHETHER JORDI LIKES OR DISLIKES THE ACTIVITY IN EACH PICTURE

Likes ☐
Dislikes ☑

1 Likes ☐
Dislikes ☑

2 Likes ☑
Dislikes ☐

3 Likes ☑
Dislikes ☐

4 Likes ☑
Dislikes ☐

10.6 READ THE JOB ADVERTISEMENT AND ANSWER THE QUESTIONS

The tour guide might work with children. True ☑ False ☐

1 Not many tourists go to Notwen Castle. True ☐ False ☑

2 The job involves greeting visitors. True ☑ False ☐

3 The tour guide must like working alone. True ☐ False ☑

4 The tour guide always works inside. True ☐ False ☑

5 The job involves weekend work. True ☑ False ☐

JOBS

Tour Guide
needed for top tourist attraction

Do you love working with people from all ages and backgrounds? Notwen Castle is one of the most popular castles in the country. Every visitor to Notwen Castle is special. It will be your job to welcome them to the castle. You must enjoy working as part of a team and have great customer service skills. The job includes working outside and on weekends.

10 ✅ CHECKLIST

⚙️ "Like," "enjoy," and "hate" ☐   **Aa** Workplace activities ☐   🧩 Finding the right job ☐

11 Describing your workplace

One way of telling people about your company is by using "there is" and "there are." Use "Is there...?" or "Are there...?" to ask questions about a workplace.

⚙ **New language** "There is" and "there are"
Aa **Vocabulary** Office equipment
🧩 **New skill** Describing a workplace

11.1 KEY LANGUAGE "THERE IS" AND "THERE ARE"

Use "there is" to talk about one thing, and "there are" to talk about more than one thing.

There is **always a supervisor on the factory floor.**

There are **six well-trained assistants on her team.**

11.2 FURTHER EXAMPLES "THERE IS" AND "THERE ARE"

There's **a business dress code at this company.**

"There is" can be shortened to "There's."

There are **two printers on your floor.**

"There are" cannot be shortened.

There isn't **a water cooler in the kitchen.**

Use "not" or its short form in negatives.

There aren't **any elevators in the office.**

Use "any" for negative plurals.

Is there **a set time for lunch breaks?**

Start questions with "Is there" or "Are there."

Are there **any files in the stationery cabinet?**

Use "any" for plurals in questions.

11.3 REWRITE THE SENTENCES, CORRECTING THE ERRORS

> There is 10 people on the sales team.
> _There are 10 people on the sales team._

1 There are'nt any bathrooms on this floor.

There aren't any bathrooms on this floor

2 Is there any stationery cabinet in the office?

Is there a stationery cabinet in the office?

3 There's staff cafeteria on the third floor.

There is a staff cafeteria on the third floor

4 There isnt an elevator in this building.

There isn't an elevator in this building

5 Is there any places to lock my bicycle here?

Is there any place to lock my bicycle here

6 Are there a desk ready for our new designer?

Is there a desk ready for our new designer

7 There're lots of envelopes in the cabinet.

There are lots of envelopes in the cabinet

🔊

11.4 LISTEN TO THE AUDIO AND WRITE ANSWERS TO THE QUESTIONS IN FULL SENTENCES

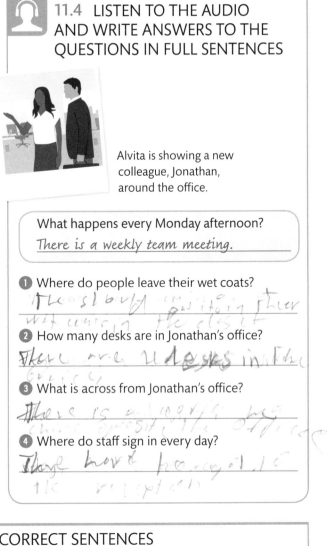

Alvita is showing a new colleague, Jonathan, around the office.

> What happens every Monday afternoon?
> _There is a weekly team meeting._

1 Where do people leave their wet coats?

People leave their wet coats in the closet

2 How many desks are in Jonathan's office?

There are 4 desks in the office

3 What is across from Jonathan's office?

There is a meeting room across the office

4 Where do staff sign in every day?

Staff sign in at the reception

11.5 USE THE CHART TO CREATE SIX CORRECT SENTENCES AND SAY THEM OUT LOUD

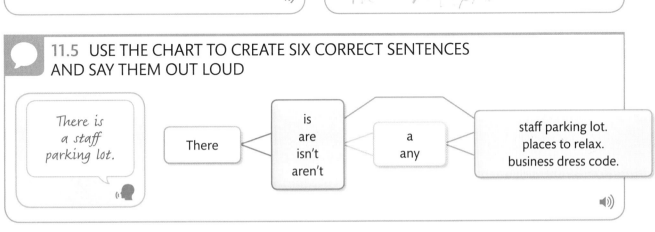

> _There is a staff parking lot._

| There | is / are / isn't / aren't | a / any | staff parking lot. / places to relax. / business dress code. |

🔊

---

11 ✓ CHECKLIST

⚙️ "There is" and "there are" ☐   **Aa** Office equipment ☐   🧩 Describing a workplace ☐

12 Vocabulary

12.1 MONEY

bills (US) / notes (UK)

coins

wallet

wallet (US) / purse (UK)

credit card

debit card

cash machine / ATM

withdraw money

bank

bank statement

online banking

mobile banking

receipt

currency

cash register (US) / till (UK)

safe

invoice

check (US) / cheque (UK)

deposit / pay in money

transfer money

46

12.2 PAY AND CONDITIONS

The company I work for pays an hourly rate of $15.

hourly rate
[the amount of money paid per hour]

The salary for this job is $35,000.

salary
[a fixed, regular payment every month, often expressed as an annual sum]

I work fewer hours now, but I had to take a huge pay cut.

a pay cut
[a reduction in pay]

My annual review was really positive so I'm hoping to get a raise next year.

a raise (US) / a pay rise (UK)
[an increase in pay]

My bonus this year was $2,000 so I'm going to buy a new car.

a bonus
[money added to a person's wages as a reward for good performance]

Benefits include a free gym membership.

benefits
[extras given to employees in addition to their usual pay]

I work extra hours regularly and get overtime pay.

overtime
[additional pay for extra hours worked]

The demand for plumbers has decreased so I earned half as much this year.

to earn
[to receive money in return for labor or services]

The shop has been really busy so our wages are increasing next week.

wage
[the amount of money paid per week or month]

I get 20 days of annual vacation every year.

annual vacation (US) / annual leave (UK)
[paid time off work granted by employers]

13 Personal qualities

You will encounter people with different skills and personalities at work. It is useful to be able to describe your co-workers and discuss their strengths and weaknesses.

🔧 **New language** Possessive adjectives
Aa Vocabulary Personality traits
🧩 **New skill** Describing your co-workers

13.1 KEY LANGUAGE ADJECTIVES

Adjectives are usually placed before nouns or after some verbs such as "be," "become," "get," "seem," and "look."

Adjective comes before the noun.

Adjective comes after the verb "be."

I run a **great** team, but John is really **lazy**. It's not **fair** on his co-workers.

TIP
Adjectives that describe negative qualities, such as "lazy," are usually avoided in business environments.

13.2 FURTHER EXAMPLES ADJECTIVES

Adjectives do not change form with feminine nouns.

Chloe is **polite** to clients.

Sally is always **calm** under pressure.

Michael is very **hardworking**.

Fatima is a **creative** designer.

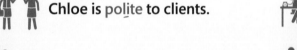
Ben seems **very organized**.

Use "very" or "really" before adjectives to add emphasis.

Ruth and Ian always look **great**.

Adjectives do not change form with plural nouns.

13.3 LISTEN TO THE AUDIO, THEN NUMBER THE PEOPLE IN THE ORDER THAT THEY ARE DESCRIBED

 Ⓐ
 Ⓑ 1
 Ⓒ
 Ⓓ 2 Ⓔ 3

POSITIVE

motivated
ambitious
helpful
bright
intelligent

NEGATIVE

impatient
lazy
impolite
nervous
boring

OUR TEAM

Career climbers who are moving up fast

Meet two of our new employees

A design that inspired Sam Riley

Sam Riley joins Scarlett Fashion Design after a short, steep climb to the top of his career ladder. Sam says, "I've always been an extremely motivated and ambitious person. I am sometimes a little impatient with lazy or impolite people, but I hope my new colleagues will find me to be helpful."

Alik Novozik already has a reputation as a bright and intelligent designer and we are very happy to welcome him to the Scarlett family. Alik says, "I'm looking forward to working with the design team here. Some people say I can be a little nervous. Even if I do get nervous sometimes, I'm definitely not boring."

 13.5 REWRITE THE SENTENCES, CORRECTING THE ERRORS

This is a team great. All my colleagues be really hardworkings.
This is a great team. All my colleagues are really hardworking.

❶ My team leader impolite is and he is also impatient very.

My team leader impolite is also he is also very impatient

❷ My co-workers say that I really motivated and ambitious am.

My co-workers that I am ... ted and amb ...

❸ The new young intern seems very intelligent and he really be polite.

The new young intern seems ve ... he really polite

❹ I'm very lucky. All my colleagues be hardworking and helpfuls.

I'm very lucky. All ... colleagues ... and helpful.

13.6 KEY LANGUAGE POSSESSIVE ADJECTIVES

Possessive adjectives tell you who something belongs to. Use them to talk about colleagues, work, or competitors.

Subject pronoun.

She looks busy.

Yes. Tamsin takes her work very seriously.

Possessive adjective means the work belongs to Tamsin.

13.7 FURTHER EXAMPLES POSSESSIVE ADJECTIVES

Your team is so hardworking.

Pablo is talking to his manager.

My staff is very motivated.

Their products aren't very good.

13.8 HOW TO FORM POSSESSIVE ADJECTIVES

SUBJECT PRONOUN	I	you	he	she	it	we	they
	⬇	⬇	⬇	⬇	⬇	⬇	⬇
POSSESSIVE ADJECTIVE	my	your	his	her	its	our	their

 13.9 FILL IN THE GAPS BY TURNING THE SUBJECT PRONOUNS INTO POSSESSIVE ADJECTIVES

Sophia is so efficient. _____*Her*_____ (She) desk is always very well organized.

❶ Two of the people on ___My___ (I) team are new to the company, but they're settling in well.

❷ ___their___ (They) manager is very good with people. They enjoy working with him.

❸ The company is very proud of ___its___ (it) reputation and quality products.

❹ Is this ___your___ (you) phone? It doesn't belong to me but I found it on my desk.

50

13.10 KEY LANGUAGE POSSESSIVE PRONOUNS

Use possessive pronouns to refer back to your achievements or the things you own. If you use the possessive pronoun, don't repeat the noun phrase in the question.

"Mine" sounds more natural than "my design."

Is that design yours? It looks great!

Yes, it's mine. I'm very proud of it.

13.11 HOW TO FORM POSSESSIVE PRONOUNS

POSSESSIVE ADJECTIVE	my	your	his	her	its	our	their
POSSESSIVE PRONOUN	mine	yours	his	hers	its	ours	theirs

13.12 CROSS OUT THE INCORRECT WORD IN EACH SENTENCE

This laptop is ~~their~~ / theirs.

1 We hate their product but we love ~~our~~ / ours.

2 They are proud of their / ~~theirs~~ project.

3 Our / ~~Ours~~ clients expect excellent service.

4 This isn't her desk. It's ~~my~~ / mine.

5 This is amazing. Is it her / ~~hers~~ project?

13.13 WRITE EACH SENTENCE IN ITS OTHER FORM

This is my computer.	This computer is mine.
1 _I think these are your file_	I think these files are yours.
2 Is this his desk?	_Is this desk his?_
3 _These are her pens_	These pens are hers.
4 Are those their products?	_Are those products theirs?_

51

13.14 KEY LANGUAGE POSSESSIVE APOSTROPHE

Add an apostrophe and the letter "s" to the end of a singular noun to show that what comes after the noun belongs to it.

Apostrophe with an "s" signifies ownership.

Jeremy is Pepe's line manager.

[Jeremy is the line manager of Pepe.]

Add an apostrophe with no "s" to plural nouns.

To show belonging with a plural noun, just add an apostrophe after the "s."

Jeremy is my colleagues' line manager.

[Jeremy is the line manager of multiple people.]

🔊

13.15 ⚠ COMMON MISTAKES POSSESSIVE APOSTROPHE

Never use an apostrophe and "s" after a plural noun in a statement which does not express possession.

"Colleagues" is a plural noun, but it does not refer to possession here.

My colleagues are late. ✓

My colleagues' are late. ✗

Don't use an apostrophe because "late" doesn't belong to "colleagues."

My colleague's are late. ✗

13.16 REWRITE THE SENTENCES, CORRECTING THE ERRORS

> Jasons assistant often works late.
> *Jason's assistant often works late.*

❶ The intern's work really hard.

the interns work really hard

❷ All the team members' are intelligent.

All the team Members are intalliget

❸ This big room is my boss office.

this big room is my boss's office

❹ All the bosses' have parking spaces.

all the bosses have parking spaces.

❺ The best thing about this product is it's strength.

the best thing about is its strength

🔊

13.17 REWRITE THE HIGHLIGHTED PHRASES, CORRECTING THE ERRORS

Performance Review:
Jorge Perez

Performance Review:
Maria Moran

Jorge is very hardworking and he confidence has grown since his joined the company last summer. He writes excellent reports and is polite and friendly with co-workers and customers. Jorges supervisor believes that he will be promoted soon and will have an excellent future in the company. We are very pleased with his work and continued progress here.

Maria does not seem to be very happy at work at the moment. She progress is slow and she has not completed a single project yet. Her main problem is that she has difficulties working as part of a team. Co-workers complain that Maria impatient is and also unfriendly. This is a shame as she is obviously intelligent very. We hope that Maria will begin to see how important it is to be a good team player.

his confidence has grown

1 *he joined the company*

2 *gorges supervior*

3 *her progress is slow*

4 *maria is impatient*

5 *very intelligent*

13.18 USE THE CHART TO CREATE 14 CORRECT SENTENCES AND SAY THEM OUT LOUD

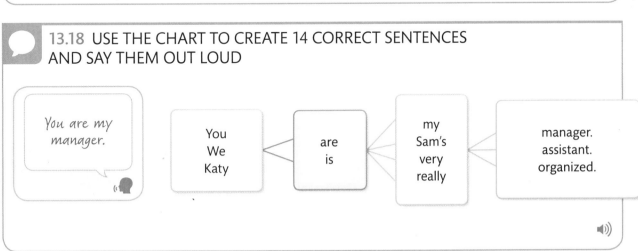

You are my manager.

| You / We / Katy | are / is | my / Sam's / very / really | manager. / assistant. / organized. |

14 Describing your job

One way of telling someone about your job is to use adjectives to describe it. Adjectives can also help you to make comparisons with other roles you have had.

⚙ **New language** Adjectives and comparatives
Aa Vocabulary Money and pay
✚ **New skill** Describing your job to someone

14.1 KEY LANGUAGE ADJECTIVES WITH "-ING" AND "-ED"

Adjectives that end in "-ing" describe the effect something has.
Adjectives ending in "-ed" describe how something is affected.

The job causes tiredness.

My job is very tiring.
I am always so tired!

The man experiences tiredness.

🔊

14.2 FURTHER EXAMPLES ADJECTIVES WITH "-ING" AND "-ED"

The building is amazing.
The tourists are amazed.

The meeting was boring.
They were bored.

The task is annoying.
She is annoyed.

The vacation is relaxing.
He is relaxed.

🔊

14.3 CROSS OUT THE INCORRECT WORD IN EACH SENTENCE

That's a very ~~interested~~ / interesting idea.

① That meeting was really ~~bored~~ / boring.

② The printer can be ~~annoyed~~ / annoying at times.

③ By the end of the week, I'm really tired / ~~tiring~~.

④ The system is confused / ~~confusing~~ at first.

⑤ I'm very excited / ~~exciting~~ about my project.

⑥ The news was ~~shocked~~ / shocking.

⑦ I was very surprised / ~~surprising~~ by my raise!

🔊

14.4 READ THE ARTICLE AND ANSWER THE QUESTIONS

Sven is self-employed.
True ☐ False ☐ Not given ☑

1 Sven wanted to work on a space station.
True ☐ False ☑ Not given ☐

2 Sven's job is based in the US.
True ☑ False ☐ Not given ☐

3 Sven thinks everyone would like to do his job.
True ☑ False ☐ Not given ☐

4 Sven works some weekends.
True ☑ False ☐ Not given ☐

5 Sven finds his work annoying.
True ☑ False ☐ Not given ☐

Reach for the stars

This week we talk to Sven about his work

I was really excited when I first got this job. More than 3,000 people applied for it and I was thrilled to be successful. I do really interesting research on astronauts and space programs. I work in a large office in the United States and analyze data from space stations and satellites. I think the work is really fascinating, although some people might think that looking at screens of statistics from space stations is quite boring. The data arrives all the time, so the work can be quite tiring. We all work quite long hours, but we never get annoyed as we hope that the work we do will be important for scientists and other researchers.

Aa 14.5 READ THE CLUES AND WRITE THE WORDS FROM THE PANEL IN THE CORRECT PLACES ON THE GRID

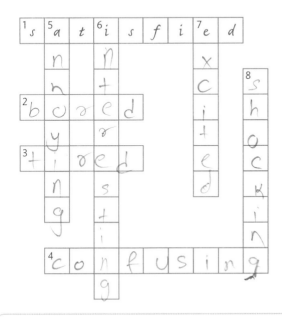

ACROSS

1 Happy or pleased with what you have.

2 Lacking interest and patience.

3 Needing sleep or rest.

4 Difficult to follow or understand.

DOWN

5 Causing irritation and frustration.

6 Something that you want to learn more about.

7 Enthusiastic and eager.

8 Unexpected, surprising, or upsetting.

bored   excited   ~~satisfied~~   tired   shocking   confusing   interesting   annoying

55

14.6 KEY LANGUAGE COMPARATIVE ADJECTIVES

Most adjectives have a comparative form that is used
to describe the difference between two things.

> **Do you like the new job?
> I bet the salary is higher!**

Add "-er" to make
the comparative.

> **It is, but the hours are much
> longer than my old job.**

Use "than" after the
comparative to compare
one thing to another.

14.7 FURTHER EXAMPLES COMPARATIVE ADJECTIVES

If the adjective ends
in "e," just add "r."

  My new office is closer to the city.

For adjectives ending in "y,"
take off the "y" and add "ier."

 I leave the house earlier now.

The New York office is bigger.

For single-syllable adjectives
ending consonant-vowel-consonant,
double the final letter and add "er."

 Tickets are more expensive.

For adjectives with more than
two syllables, use "more" to
make the comparative.

Adjective
does not
change.

 14.8 FILL IN THE GAPS WITH THE CORRECT COMPARATIVES

My new commute is ___more expensive___ (expensive) than before, and it's ___longer___ (long).

❶ This printer is _____ (fast) than the other, but that one is _____ (reliable).

❷ This coffee is _____ (strong) than I normally buy, but it is also _____ (tasty).

❸ This building is _____ (new) than my last workplace, and the area is _____ (quiet).

❹ This café is _____ (busy) than the other one, so the service is _____ (slow).

❺ My new uniform is _____ (comfortable) than my old one, but _____ (ugly).

14.9 KEY LANGUAGE IRREGULAR COMPARATIVE ADJECTIVES

Some common adjectives (usually short words)
have comparatives that do not follow the rules.

ADJECTIVE	bad	good	well	far
↓	↓	↓	↓	↓
COMPARATIVE	worse	better	better	farther (US) further (UK)

"Well" as an adjective means healthy; "better"
here means "healthier" or "no longer ill."

◀))

14.10 MARK THE SENTENCES THAT ARE CORRECT

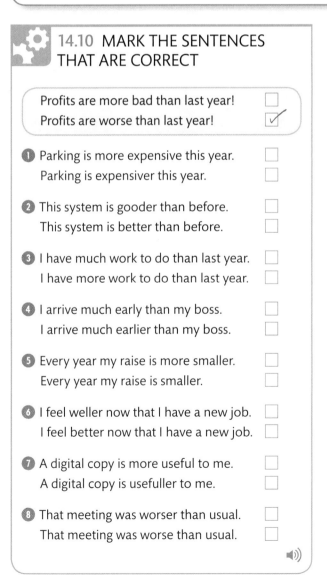

Profits are more bad than last year! ☐
Profits are worse than last year! ☑

① Parking is more expensive this year. ☐
Parking is expensiver this year. ☐

② This system is gooder than before. ☐
This system is better than before. ☐

③ I have much work to do than last year. ☐
I have more work to do than last year. ☐

④ I arrive much early than my boss. ☐
I arrive much earlier than my boss. ☐

⑤ Every year my raise is more smaller. ☐
Every year my raise is smaller. ☐

⑥ I feel weller now that I have a new job. ☐
I feel better now that I have a new job. ☐

⑦ A digital copy is more useful to me. ☐
A digital copy is usefuller to me. ☐

⑧ That meeting was worser than usual. ☐
That meeting was worse than usual. ☐

◀))

14.11 LISTEN TO THE AUDIO AND MATCH THE IMAGES TO THE CORRECT PHRASES

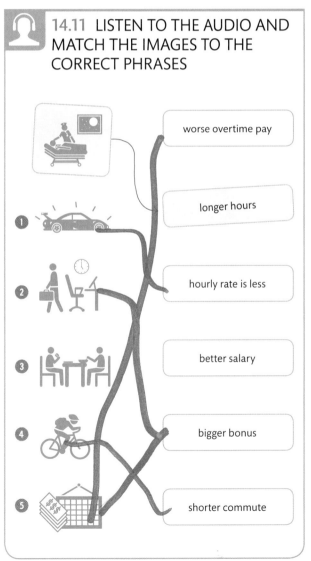

worse overtime pay

longer hours

hourly rate is less

better salary

bigger bonus

shorter commute

Aa 14.12 MATCH THE WORDS TO THEIR OPPOSITES

less		stronger
① difficult		worse
② excited		more
③ weaker		bored
④ higher		large
⑤ expensive		lower
⑥ lighter		heavier
⑦ bigger		easy
⑧ little		cheap
⑨ better		smaller

🔊

14.13 REWRITE THE HIGHLIGHTED PHRASES, CORRECTING ERRORS

Join our team

Are you **more efficienter** than your colleagues? Are you more **friendlier than** others? And do you want to be **more successfuller?** ...then come to work with us at Sandwich Delicious. We sell **morer** sandwiches than any other sandwich bar in the city. We also offer **more good** pay than similar jobs in the area. All our co-workers at Sandwich Delicious deli get **more long** vacations than those working at similar companies. You will get three days off every week.

more efficient	③ _____
① _____	④ _____
② _____	⑤ _____

14.14 MATCH THE BEGINNINGS OF THE SENTENCES TO THE CORRECT ENDINGS

This project is more interesting	tastier than restaurant meals.
① Now, my vacations are longer	efficient than the old one.
② This new computer system is more	than the last one.
③ These presentations are making me more	lighter than the old ones.
④ These new laptops are	than they used to be.
⑤ The cafeteria lunches are	bored than yesterday's.

🔊

14.15 LISTEN TO THE AUDIO AND ANSWER THE QUESTIONS

Joe is talking about his new job and comparing it to the previous company where he worked.

Joe says the new company is more modern.
True ☑ False ☐ Not given ☐

1 Joe does not enjoy working in social media.
True ☐ False ☐ Not given ☑

2 Joe earns more money now than he did before.
True ☑ False ☐ Not given ☐

3 Joe spends more time at work now than before.
True ☐ False ☑ Not given ☐

4 Joe is bored in his new job.
True ☑ False ☐ Not given ☐

5 Joe's new boss has regular meetings with him.
True ☑ False ☐ Not given ☐

6 Joe's old workplace was not very organized.
True ☐ False ☑ Not given ☐

7 Joe's new workplace is more efficient.
True ☑ False ☐ Not given ☐

---

14 ⊘ CHECKLIST

⚙ Adjectives and comparatives ☐   **Aa** Money and pay ☐   🧩 Describing your job to someone ☐

♻ REVIEW THE ENGLISH YOU HAVE LEARNED IN UNITS 8–14

NEW LANGUAGE	SAMPLE SENTENCE	☑	UNIT
TALKING ABOUT YOUR SKILLS AND EXPERIENCE	I have **excellent negotiation skills.** I work in a **busy restaurant.**	☐	8.1, 8.6
LIKES AND DISLIKES	I hate **computers.** He likes giving **presentations.**	☐	10.1, 10.2
DESCRIBING A WORKPLACE	There is **a formal dress code at this company.** There are **two printers on your floor.**	☐	11.1, 11.2
DESCRIBING COLLEAGUES	Your **new team is really hard-working.** Jeremy is Pepe's **line manager.**	☐	13.1, 13.11
DESCRIBING YOUR JOB	My job is very tiring. **I am always so** tired!	☐	14.1
MAKING COMPARISONS	Is the salary higher **in your new job?**	☐	14.6

15 Workplace routines

Employees have schedules and workplaces also have their own routines and timetables. It is useful to be able to talk to colleagues about when things usually happen.

🔧 New language Prepositions of time
Aa Vocabulary Commuting and transportation
🧩 New skill Describing routines

15.1 KEY LANGUAGE PREPOSITIONS OF TIME

Use prepositions to give more information about when something happens.

"On" is often used before days and dates to say when something happens.

"At" is used to say what time something happens.

There is a staff meeting on Mondays at 10 o'clock.

When you use "on" with a day of the week, add "–s" to the day to show that the thing happens regularly.

15.2 KEY LANGUAGE MORE PREPOSITIONS OF TIME

Use "by" to say when something will be completed. It means "before."

"Before" describes something that happens prior to something else.

"After" refers to an event that follows something else.

I need to finish this by 3pm.

I can't do it before I take my break.

After my break I have to clear up.

NOW   3PM   BREAK

15.3 REWRITE THE SENTENCES, PUTTING THE WORDS IN THE CORRECT ORDER

| I | home | work | Fridays. | from | on |

I work from home on Fridays.

2 | leave | Mr. | Don't | Davies. | before |

Mr. Davies. Don't Leave before.

1 | served | is | at | noon. | Lunch |

is served Lunch at noon

3 | arrive | Never | 9am. | after |

After 9am. Never arrive.

15.4 KEY LANGUAGE PREPOSITIONS SHOWING DURATION

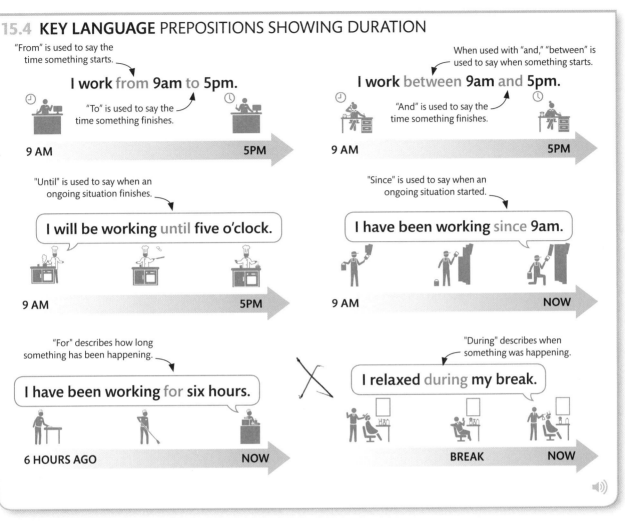

"From" is used to say the time something starts.

I work from 9am to 5pm.

"To" is used to say the time something finishes.

9 AM   5PM

When used with "and," "between" is used to say when something starts.

I work between 9am and 5pm.

"And" is used to say the time something finishes.

9 AM   5PM

"Until" is used to say when an ongoing situation finishes.

I will be working until five o'clock.

9 AM   5PM

"Since" is used to say when an ongoing situation started.

I have been working since 9am.

9 AM   NOW

"For" describes how long something has been happening.

I have been working for six hours.

6 HOURS AGO   NOW

"During" describes when something was happening.

I relaxed during my break.

BREAK   NOW

15.5 CROSS OUT THE INCORRECT WORD IN EACH SENTENCE, THEN SAY THE SENTENCES OUT LOUD

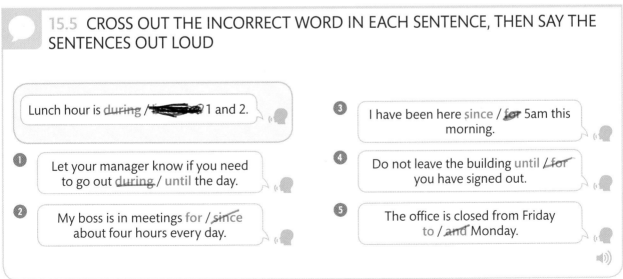

Lunch hour is during / ~~between~~ 1 and 2.

❸ I have been here since / ~~for~~ 5am this morning.

❶ Let your manager know if you need to go out ~~during~~ / until the day.

❹ Do not leave the building until / ~~for~~ you have signed out.

❷ My boss is in meetings for / ~~since~~ about four hours every day.

❺ The office is closed from Friday to / ~~and~~ Monday.

61

15.6 KEY LANGUAGE GETTING TO WORK

There are a number of ways to describe how you get to work.

Use "take" and "catch" with forms of transportation that you do not drive or control.

I walk **to work.**

I cycle **to work.**

I drive **to work.**

I take the **metro**

15.7 MATCH THE PAIRS OF PHRASES THAT MEAN THE SAME THING

I drive to work. — I go by car.

1 I take the metro to work. — I go by metro.

2 I cycle to work in good weather. — Sometimes I ride my bike to work.

3 I commute by train. — I go by train to work.

4 I usually walk to work. — I normally go to work on foot.

5 When it rains, I go by taxi. — Sometimes I take a taxi to work.

6 I catch the bus to work. — I take the bus.

🔊

15.8 CROSS OUT INCORRECT WORD IN EACH SENTENCE

 I usually take / ~~drive~~ the bus to work.

1 I always catch / drive to work.

2 It's usually quicker to bike / cycle.

3 When it's sunny, we go on foot / walk.

4 I don't like taking the metro / cycle.

5 I walk / foot to work to stay fit.

6 I read a book when I go on / by train.

7 I take / walk the bus when it rains.

🔊

You can't "take" or "catch" a car or a bike as these are things you control yourself.

I catch the bus.

Use "go by" + the means of transportation. The exception is "go on foot."

I go by train.

15.9 LISTEN TO THE AUDIO, THEN NUMBER THE PICTURES IN THE ORDER THEY ARE DESCRIBED

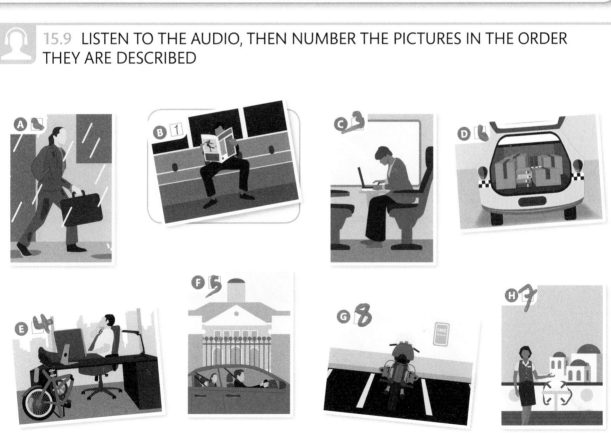

16 Vocabulary

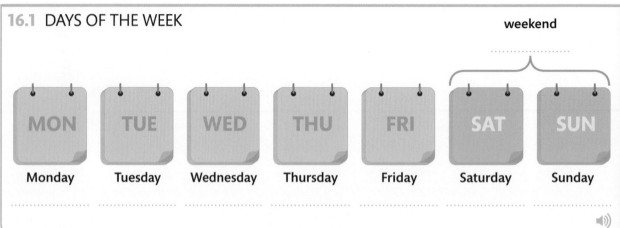

16.1 DAYS OF THE WEEK

weekend

MON	TUE	WED	THU	FRI	SAT	SUN
Monday	Tuesday	Wednesday	Thursday	Friday	Saturday	Sunday

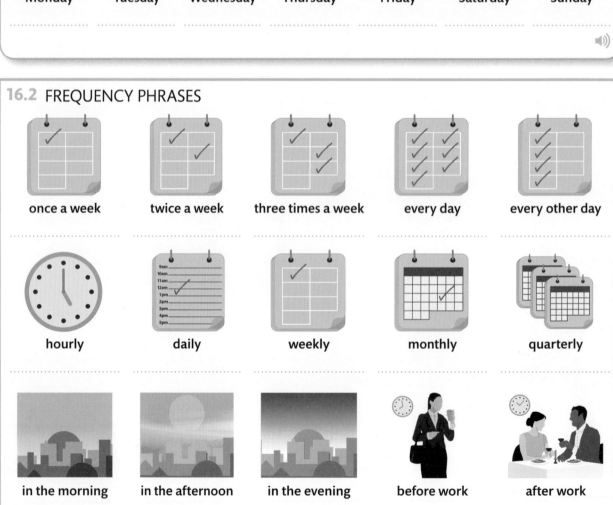

16.2 FREQUENCY PHRASES

once a week   twice a week   three times a week   every day   every other day

hourly   daily   weekly   monthly   quarterly

in the morning   in the afternoon   in the evening   before work   after work

16.3 FREE TIME

 read

 draw

 write

 cook

 take photos

 stay (at) home

 listen to music

 watch television

 watch a movie

 see a play

 visit a museum / art gallery

 meet friends

 go out for a meal

 go shopping

 go to the gym

 go cycling

 walk / hike

 go running

 go camping

do exercise

 play sports

play board games

 play video games

 play an instrument

 do yoga

65

17 Hobbies and habits

When talking with colleagues about your hobbies and habits, you may want to use adverbs of frequency to say how often you do the activities.

⚙ **New language** Adverbs of frequency
Aa Vocabulary Hobbies and habits
🧩 **New skill** Talking about free time

17.1 **VOCABULARY** ADVERBS OF FREQUENCY

Some adverbs tell you how frequently something happens.
"Always" and "never" are definite. Others, like "sometimes," are less specific.
Their position in a sentence depends on the main verbs and auxiliaries.

 100%

I **always** go to the gym after work.

Adverbs go after the verb "be."

I am **usually** happy to stay at home in the evening.

Adverbs go before other main verbs.

My company **frequently** organizes sponsored walks.

I **often** play computer games at home.

"Sometimes" and "often" can also go at the beginning or end of the sentence.

My team goes out for a meal **sometimes**.

My wife and I **occasionally** go cycling together.

I **rarely** work weekends if I have a choice.

0%

I have **never** played golf with my boss. I'm terrible at it!

Adverbs go between an auxiliary and the main verb.

🔊

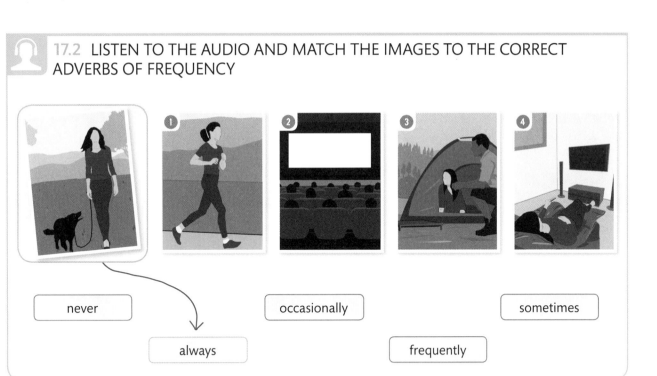

17.2 LISTEN TO THE AUDIO AND MATCH THE IMAGES TO THE CORRECT ADVERBS OF FREQUENCY

never

occasionally

sometimes

always

frequently

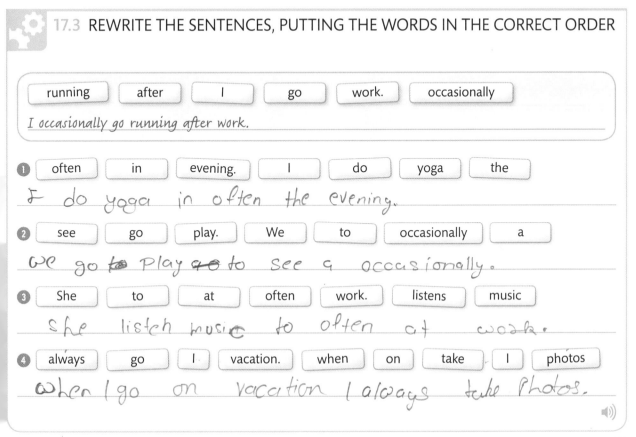

17.3 REWRITE THE SENTENCES, PUTTING THE WORDS IN THE CORRECT ORDER

running | after | I | go | work. | occasionally

I occasionally go running after work.

1. often | in | evening. | I | do | yoga | the

I do yoga in often the evening.

2. see | go | play. | We | to | occasionally | a

We go to Play to see a occasionally.

3. She | to | at | often | work. | listens | music

She listen music to often at work.

4. always | go | I | vacation. | when | on | take | I | photos

when I go on vacation I always take Photos.

67

17.4 KEY LANGUAGE SUPERLATIVE ADJECTIVES

Superlative adjectives are used to compare two or more objects, people, or places. The superlative describes the most extreme.

"The" is used before a superlative.

Friday nights are always the loudest.

This is the most interesting gallery in town.

Long adjectives take "the most" or "the least" before the adjective to form the superlative.

17.5 HOW TO FORM SUPERLATIVE ADJECTIVES

For most short adjectives, "-est" is added to make the superlative. There are different spelling rules depending on the ending of the simple form of the adjective.

large

largest

If the adjective ends in "-e," "-st" is added.

easy

easiest

For some adjectives ending in "-y," the "-y" is removed and "-iest" added.

hot

hottest

For adjectives ending consonant-vowel-consonant, the last letter is doubled and "-est" is added.

17.6 FURTHER EXAMPLES SUPERLATIVE ADJECTIVES

 That's the longest run I've ever done!

 The earliest train is at 4am.

 That's the most expensive item!

 I go to the newest gym in town.

 This is the biggest launch to date.

 It's the least exciting party ever.

"The least" has the opposite meaning from "the most."

17.7 KEY LANGUAGE IRREGULAR SUPERLATIVE ADJECTIVES

Some common adjectives (usually short words) have superlatives that do not follow the rules.

ADJECTIVE	bad	good	little	much	far
	↓	↓	↓	↓	↓
SUPERLATIVE	worst	best	least	most	farthest (US) furthest (UK)

◀))

17.8 MARK THE SENTENCES THAT ARE CORRECT

This is the best restaurant in town. ☑
This is the most good restaurant in town. ☐

❶ This is the most good book I've ever read. ☐
This is the best book I've ever read. ☐

❷ The piano is most easy instrument to play. ☐
The piano is the easiest instrument to play. ☐

❸ Yannick listens to the most loud music. ☐
Yannick listens to the loudest music. ☐

❹ Shopping is the expensivest hobby I do. ☐
Shopping is the most expensive hobby I do. ☐

❺ That was the baddest play I have ever seen. ☐
That was the worst play I have ever seen. ☐

❻ Exercising is the more relaxing thing I do. ☐
Exercising is the most relaxing thing I do. ☐

❼ Let's eat at the most close restaurant. ☐
Let's eat at the closest restaurant. ☐

◀))

17.9 CROSS OUT THE INCORRECT WORDS IN EACH SENTENCE, THEN SAY THE SENTENCES OUT LOUD

The earliest / ~~most early~~ yoga class is at 8am.

❶ The interestingest / most interesting gallery I've been to is in Paris.

❷ I've just finished the worst / most bad book I've ever read.

❸ The most long / longest hike I've ever done is 15km.

❹ The farthest / most far I've ever gone cycling is 50 miles.

❺ I think that hiking is the morest exciting / most exciting hobby.

◀))

18 Past events

The past simple is often used when talking with co-workers about events that started and finished at a specific time in the recent or distant past.

⚙ **New language** The past simple
Aa Vocabulary Activities outside work
🧩 **New skill** Talking about past events

18.1 KEY LANGUAGE REGULAR VERBS IN THE PAST SIMPLE

The past simple describes events that happened in the past. The past simple forms of regular verbs end in "-ed." The negative uses "did not" plus the base form of the main verb.

I watched **the game last night. It was great!**

I didn't watch **the game. I stayed at work late.**

18.2 HOW TO FORM REGULAR VERBS IN THE PAST SIMPLE

The past forms of most verbs do not change with the subject.

Use the same form for all subjects.

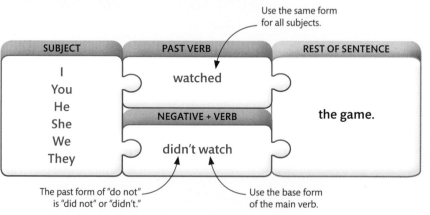

SUBJECT	PAST VERB	REST OF SENTENCE
I You He She We They	watched	the game.
	NEGATIVE + VERB	
	didn't watch	

The past form of "do not" is "did not" or "didn't."

Use the base form of the main verb.

18.3 FURTHER EXAMPLES REGULAR VERBS IN THE PAST SIMPLE

He walked **to the office.**

She didn't walk **downtown.**

They arrived **together.**

We didn't arrive **on time.**

18.4 MARK THE SENTENCES THAT ARE CORRECT

They didn't stay for long. ✓
They didn't stayed for long. ☐

① I played soccer after work last night. ☐
I playd soccer after work last night. ☐

② He didn't walked to work today. ☐
He didn't walk to work today. ☐

③ I works from 9 to 5 yesterday. ☐
I worked from 9 to 5 yesterday. ☐

④ She lived in Paris for four years. ☐
She lives in Paris for four years. ☐

⑤ I talked to lots of people on my trip. ☐
I did talk to lots of people on my trip. ☐

18.5 KEY LANGUAGE SPELLING RULES FOR THE PAST SIMPLE

The past simple of all regular verbs ends in "-ed," but for some verbs, there are some spelling changes, too.

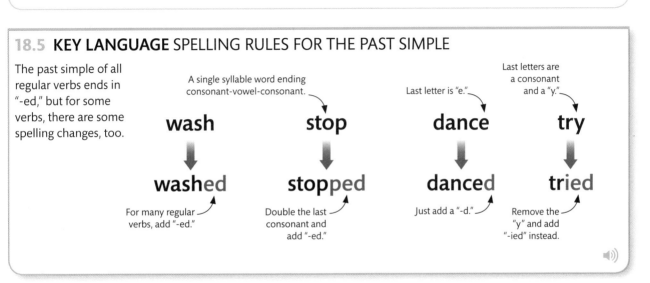

A single syllable word ending consonant-vowel-consonant.

Last letter is "e."

Last letters are a consonant and a "y."

wash → **washed**
For many regular verbs, add "-ed."

stop → **stopped**
Double the last consonant and add "-ed."

dance → **danced**
Just add a "-d."

try → **tried**
Remove the "y" and add "-ied" instead.

18.6 FILL IN THE GAPS BY PUTTING THE VERBS IN THE PAST SIMPLE

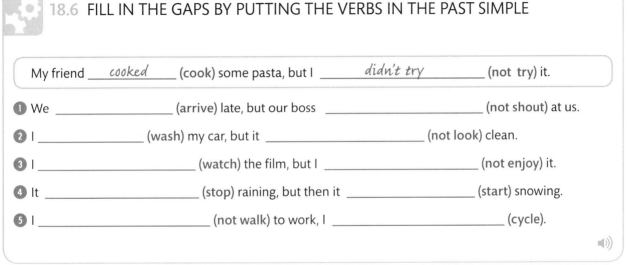

My friend ___cooked___ (cook) some pasta, but I ___didn't try___ (not try) it.

① We _____ (arrive) late, but our boss _____ (not shout) at us.

② I _____ (wash) my car, but it _____ (not look) clean.

③ I _____ (watch) the film, but I _____ (not enjoy) it.

④ It _____ (stop) raining, but then it _____ (start) snowing.

⑤ I _____ (not walk) to work, I _____ (cycle).

71

18.7 HOW TO FORM QUESTIONS IN THE PAST SIMPLE

Use "did" plus the base form of the verb
to ask a question in the past simple.

They played tennis after work.

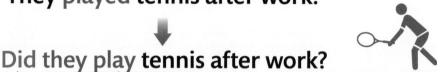

Did they play tennis after work?

"Did" goes before
the subject.

The main verb
is in its base form.

18.8 HOW TO FORM QUESTIONS IN THE PAST SIMPLE

"DID"	SUBJECT	BASE FORM OF VERB	REST OF SENTENCE
Did	they	play	tennis after work?

 ## 18.9 REWRITE THE SENTENCES AS QUESTIONS IN THE PAST SIMPLE

He visited the art gallery with his family yesterday.
Did he visit the art gallery with his family yesterday?

① You played board games when you were young.

_____

② He cooked some pasta for lunch.

_____

③ She stayed at home and watched TV last night.

_____

④ They watched a scary movie at the movie theater.

_____

⑤ They walked home from work together.

_____

Two colleagues, Jasmine and Marilyn, are talking about events from the week before.

On vacation, Jasmine watched a lot of movies.
True ☐   False ☐   Not given ✓

❸ Jasmine didn't try yoga.
True ☐   False ☐   Not given ✓

❶ Jasmine played tennis and volleyball on vacation.
True ☐   False ✓   Not given ☐

❹ Jasmine liked the local food.
True ✓   False ☐   Not given ☐

❷ Jasmine played four new sports.
True ✓   False ☐   Not given ☐

❺ Jasmine and Marilyn often cook for each other.
True ☐   False ✓   Not given ☐

18.11 DESCRIBE WHAT EACH PERSON DID, SPEAKING OUT LOUD AND USING THE PAST SIMPLE FORM OF THE VERBS IN THE PANEL

He played soccer.

❶ ~~try~~ visit a museum
~~listen to music~~

❷ listen to music

❸ Watch TV

❹ Cook a meal

❺ Play a board game

listen to music   play soccer   play a board game   cook a meal   watch TV   visit a museum

18 ✓ CHECKLIST

⚙ The past simple ☐   Aa Activities outside work ☐   Talking about past events ☐

19 Dates and times

When making arrangements or talking about past or future events, it is important to talk about the time correctly. There are a number of ways to do this in English.

⚙ **New language** When things happen
Aa Vocabulary Telling the time
🧩 **New skill** Making appointments

19.1 KEY LANGUAGE TELLING THE TIME

In spoken English, there are a few different key phrases that can be used to say what the time is.

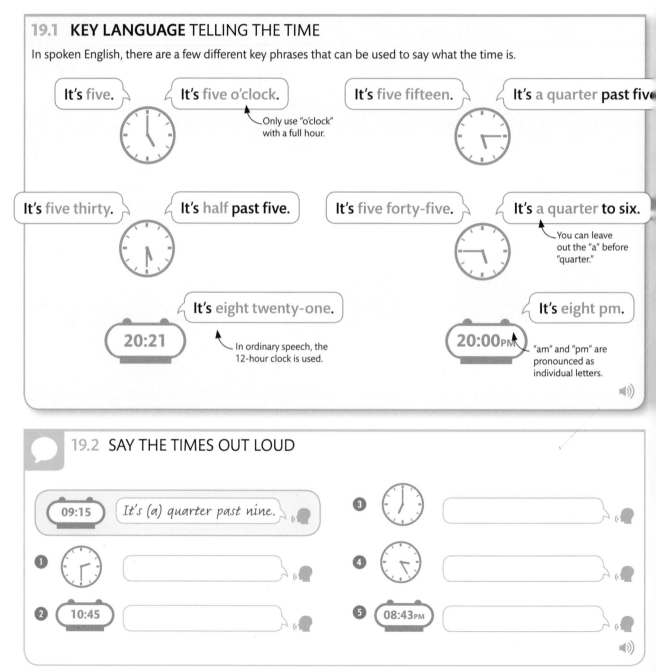

It's five.

It's five o'clock.
Only use "o'clock" with a full hour.

It's five fifteen.

It's a quarter **past five**

It's five thirty.

It's **half** past five.

It's five forty-five.

It's a quarter **to six.**
You can leave out the "a" before "quarter."

It's eight twenty-one.
20:21
In ordinary speech, the 12-hour clock is used.

It's eight pm.
20:00PM
"am" and "pm" are pronounced as individual letters.

19.2 SAY THE TIMES OUT LOUD

09:15 — It's (a) quarter past nine.

1

2 10:45

3

4

5 08:43PM

19.3 VOCABULARY MONTHS OF THE YEAR

Jan — January

Feb — February

Mar — March

Apr — April

May — May

Jun — June

Jul — July

Aug — August

Sept — September

Oct — October

Nov — November

Dec — December

19.4 KEY LANGUAGE DATES AND YEARS

In the US, people often describe dates by writing cardinal numbers and saying ordinal numbers. In the UK, people use ordinal numbers to write and say dates.

In US English, the number is written after the month.

May tenth

May the tenth

May 10 (US)
May 10th / 10th May (UK)
the 10th of May (UK / US)

the tenth of May

Most years are spoken as pairs of numbers, such as "nineteen" and "seventy-five."

nineteen seventy-five

1975

twenty fifteen

2015

You can also say, "two thousand and..." for years between 2000 and 2019.

19.5 LISTEN TO THE AUDIO AND ANSWER THE QUESTIONS

When did Joe move to London?
2010 ☐ 2011 ☐ 2012 ☑

① Joe started work in London in...
April ☐ May ☐ March ☐

② Joe first worked with Ailsa in...
April ☐ August ☐ September ☐

③ What year did they get married?
2012 ☐ 2014 ☐ 2016 ☐

④ What date is their baby due?
May 12 ☐ May 10 ☐ May 21 ☐

19 ✓ CHECKLIST

⚙ When things happen ☐   **Aa** Telling the time ☐   🧩 Making appointments ☐

20 Career history

When you meet new co-workers or attend an interview, people may ask about your previous jobs. It is important to use correct verb forms when talking about the past.

⚙ **New language** Past simple irregular verbs
Aa Vocabulary Jobs and workplaces
🧩 **New skill** Talking about previous jobs

20.1 KEY LANGUAGE PAST SIMPLE IRREGULAR VERBS

Many common English verbs have irregular forms in the past simple. The verb "be" changes form in the past depending on the subject.

> What did you do before?

> I was a waitress in a café. My co-workers were really nice.

Past simple form of the verb "be" with "I," "he," "she," and "it."

Past simple form of the verb "be" with "you," "we," and "they."

20.2 FURTHER EXAMPLES PAST SIMPLE IRREGULAR VERBS

Other past simple irregular verbs do not change form with the subject.

We had a very demanding boss.

He got very tired working night shifts.

I spent all day stacking shelves.

I left my job because it was badly paid.

Jo met our new clients yesterday.

They went on a business trip to Paris.

Past simple verbs do not change form in the third person.

20.3 KEY LANGUAGE PAST SIMPLE IRREGULAR VERBS

BASE FORM	be	have	spend	meet	get	leave	go
PAST SIMPLE	was/were	had	spent	met	got	left	went

20.4 FILL IN THE GAPS BY PUTTING THE VERBS IN THE PAST SIMPLE

My first job _____was_____ (be) in a busy restaurant kitchen.

1 When I was a gardener, I _____ (spend) the majority of my time outside.

2 I _____ (meet) lots of famous people when I worked as a reporter.

3 Benjamin _____ (go) to nearly 100 countries as a pilot.

4 In his last job, he _____ (have) a dog as a partner.

20.5 MATCH THE QUESTIONS TO THE CORRECT ANSWERS

Why did you leave your first job?

1 What did you wear in your first job?

2 What was the best thing about being a DJ?

3 How did you get a job as a chef?

4 Where did you work as a tour guide?

I met lots of famous musicians.

I spent a lot of time in museums.

I left it because it was boring.

As a police officer, I had a uniform.

I went to catering school.

20.6 LISTEN TO THE AUDIO, THEN NUMBER THE PICTURES IN THE ORDER THEY ARE DESCRIBED

A ☐

B 1

C ☐

D ☐

E ☐

20.7 READ THE ARTICLE AND WRITE ANSWERS TO THE QUESTIONS AS FULL SENTENCES

BUSINESS BULLETIN

Sadim Nalik: Mailroom to boardroom

He started in the mailroom at his father's company, but Sadim Nalik is now a respected business executive. He tells us what he learned from his first job.

I always wanted to work in my father's company, but my father told me that I had to go to college first. He always said that education was the most important thing in life. He taught himself to read and write and wanted the very best for me. I chose to study engineering in college. When I left college with a top degree, I thought that my father would give me a good job in his company. I remember he sent me an email congratulating me on my university success and offering me a job in the mailroom at the company. I felt really angry at the time because I wanted a better job. I wrote to my father that I would look for a job at another company. He then called me and said I could one day be CEO, but only if I knew the company from top to bottom. After the mailroom, I worked in the kitchen, in the HR department, as a personal assistant, and as his deputy CEO. I finally understood what hard work was like in different areas of the company. The experience taught me to respect all employees and understand that every part of the company must be working well for the whole company to succeed. My father made me CEO five years ago and my daughter, Myra, began working in the mailroom two months ago.

What did Sadim's father tell him to do?

He told Sadim to go to college.

① What did Sadim choose to study in college?

Sadim choose to study engineering in college.

② What did Sadim think his father would do?

③ Why did Sadim feel angry?

④ What did Sadim write to his father?

⑤ What did his father say he could be one day?

⑥ What did Sadim finally understand?

⑦ What did Sadim's work experience teach him?

⑧ When did Sadim's father make him CEO?

⑨ When did Myra begin working in the mailroom?

20.8 REWRITE THE SENTENCES, CORRECTING THE ERRORS

I choosed to study medical science in college.
I chose to study medical science in college.

❶ I feeled really happy when I left college with a top degree.

_____

❷ My manager sayed that one day I could be CEO of the whole company.

_____

❸ My tutor teached me that it was important to check my own work.

_____

❹ I maked my girlfriend a big cake to celebrate her new job.

_____

20.9 RESPOND TO THE AUDIO, SPEAKING OUT LOUD

What was your first job?
> *I was a sales assistant.*

❸ Why did you choose your first job?
> *because of my futual*

❶ How did you get your first job?
>

❹ When did you leave your first job?
> *7th july 2023*

❷ How did you feel on your first day?
> *I am feel better*

❺ Why did you leave your first job?
> *Personal reason.*

20 ✓ CHECKLIST

⚙ Past simple irregular verbs ☐   **Aa** Jobs and workplaces ☐   ⟐ Talking about previous jobs ☐

79

21 Company history

The past simple can be used to describe repeated or single actions in a company's history. These actions can last for a short or long time.

⚙ **New language** Past simple with time markers
Aa Vocabulary Describing trends
🧩 **New skill** Describing a company's history

21.1 KEY LANGUAGE THE PAST SIMPLE WITH TIME MARKERS

To talk about specific events in the past, such as landmarks in a company's history, use the past simple with a time marker.

I founded Transtech in 1996.

Past simple of the verb "to found," which means "to set up a company."

Time markers specify when an event happened.

21.2 FURTHER EXAMPLES THE PAST SIMPLE WITH TIME MARKERS

Time markers can go at the start of a sentence.

At first, we only had five employees.

We launched a new range of laptops last year.

Time markers that are adverbs go immediately before the verb.

"Ago" means "before now."

Ten years ago, we opened a new flagship store.

We recently merged with Alphaelectrics.

21.3 FILL IN THE GAPS USING THE WORDS IN THE PANEL

At ___*first*___ , we only sold products in store, but now we sell online.

1 We opened our tenth store two months ___*ago*___ .

2 The company ___*recently*___ merged with one of its competitors.

3 Jane Hunt opened the first Hunt Bags store ___*in*___ 1995.

4 A new CEO started working here ___*last*___ year.

last

recently

ago

~~first~~

in

21.4 LISTEN TO THE AUDIO, THEN NUMBER THE SENTENCES IN THE ORDER YOU HEAR THEM

A CEO is giving a presentation on the company history.

A At first, business was quite slow and the salon was often empty. ☐

B They opened a second hair salon in London in 1988. ☐

C By 1995, they were stylists for many top celebrities. ☐

D Brisar Styling was founded by Brian and Sarah Paterson in 1984. ☐ 1

E Five years later, they launched their hair product range. ☐

F Last year, Brisar Styling merged with our beauty product company, Wilson's. ☐

21.5 READ THE ARTICLE AND ANSWER THE QUESTIONS

> What did Cake & Crumb report last year?
>
> *It reported a record rise in profits.*

① When did Ahmed found Cake & Crumb?

_____

② Where did Ahmed work at first?

_____

③ What were sales like in the company's first year?

_____

④ When did the company open its first store?

_____

⑤ When did Cake & Crumb employ 2,000 bakers?

_____

⑥ What happened two years ago?

_____

BUSINESS WORLD

A slice of the market

This week, we look at the history of Cake & Crumb

CAKE & CRUMB IS NOW one of the biggest and most popular bakeries in the US. Last year, the company reported a record rise in profits. But Cake & Crumb had much smaller beginnings.

Ahmed Hassan founded the company in 2003. At first, Ahmed worked from his kitchen in his small apartment and sold cakes to customers online. In the company's first year, sales remained steady, but in 2005, sales increased and Ahmed opened the first Cake & Crumb store.

Now, the company has stores all over the US. By 2010, Cake & Crumb employed 2,000 bakers. Two years ago, the company launched a catering service for children's parties. With the launch of this service and rebranding, Cake & Crumb became one of the most successful companies in the catering industry.

21.6 KEY LANGUAGE DESCRIBING TRENDS

English also uses the past simple with time markers to describe business trends.
Note that some verbs for describing trends have irregular past simple forms.

Ice cream sales { increased / went up / rose } over the summer.

"Rise" has an irregular past simple form.

House prices { stayed the same / remained steady / stabilized } during the last quarter.

Demand for new cars { decreased / went down / fell } last year.

"Fall" is also an irregular verb.

 ## 21.7 FILL IN THE GAPS BY PUTTING THE VERBS IN THE PAST SIMPLE

Visitor numbers at the luxury hotel _____*fell*_____ (fall) by 20 percent last year.

1 The number of people going to festivals ~~get up~~ (go up) last year.

2 Fortunately, the cost of fuel for transportation _____ (stabilize) recently.

3 In the really wet summer of 2010, sales of umbrellas _____ (rise) a lot.

4 The number of people downloading music _____ (stay the same) last month.

5 The numbers of students earning MBAs _____ (remain steady) last year.

21.8 CROSS OUT THE INCORRECT WORDS IN EACH SENTENCE, THEN SAY THE SENTENCES OUT LOUD

Our sales figures ~~increased up~~ / went up in 2011, but ~~falled~~ / fell in 2012.

1 At / In first, the value of the company stayed / stay the same.

2 Marketing costs increasing / increased and sales also rose / rosing.

3 Last / Recent summer, umbrella sales increased / increasing because it was rainy.

4 The number of customers decrease / decreased, but profits go / went up.

5 Two years ago / past, we launched an online delivery service and our sales rised / rose.

---

21 ✓ CHECKLIST

⚙ Past simple with time markers ☐   **Aa** Describing trends ☐   🧩 Describing a company's history ☐

🔄 REVIEW THE ENGLISH YOU HAVE LEARNED IN UNITS 15-21

NEW LANGUAGE	SAMPLE SENTENCE	☑	UNIT
PREPOSITIONS OF TIME AND DURATION	There is a staff meeting on Mondays. I work from 9am to 5pm.	☐	15.1, 15.4
ADVERBS OF FREQUENCY	I always go to the gym after work.	☐	17.1
SUPERLATIVE ADJECTIVES	Friday nights are always the loudest.	☐	17.4
PAST SIMPLE	I watched the game last night. Did they play tennis after work?	☐	18.1, 18.7
PAST SIMPLE IRREGULAR VERBS	I was a waitress. We had a very demanding boss.	☐	20.1, 20.2
PAST SIMPLE WITH TIME MARKERS	I founded Transtech in 1996.	☐	21.1, 21.2

22 Vocabulary

22.1 MAKING ARRANGEMENTS

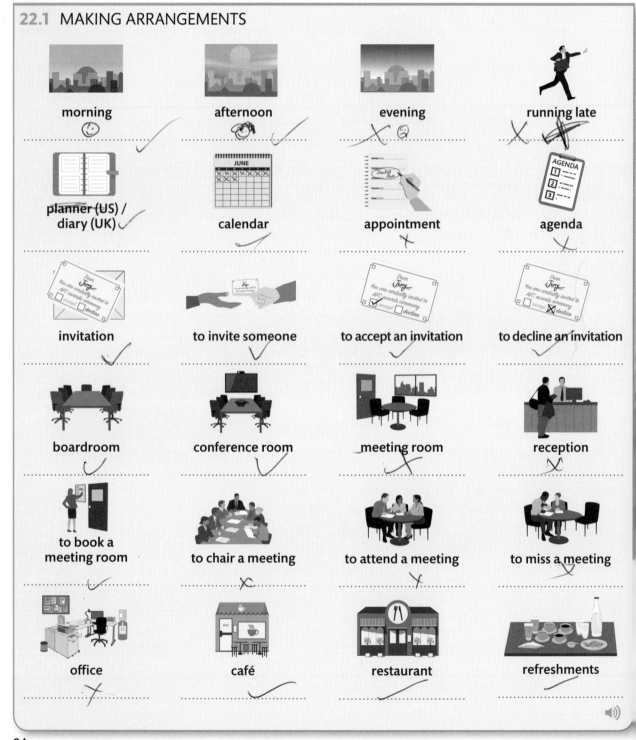

morning

afternoon

evening

running late

planner (US) / diary (UK)

calendar

appointment

agenda

invitation

to invite someone

to accept an invitation

to decline an invitation

boardroom

conference room

meeting room

reception

to book a meeting room

to chair a meeting

to attend a meeting

to miss a meeting

office

café

restaurant

refreshments

22.2 ACCEPTING AND DECLINING

I'm afraid I'm busy today.

to be busy
[to have lots to do]

10am is good for me. See you then!

good for me
[I am free at that time]

Yes, I am free on Wednesday and Thursday this week.

to be free
[to be available]

Yes, the café suits me.

to suit someone
[to be convenient]

I can't make the meeting on Monday. I will reschedule it for Tuesday.

to reschedule
[to decide on a new time and date for a meeting]

2pm is fine. I look forward to meeting you then.

to look forward to
[to be pleased about something that is going to happen]

I'm really busy this morning. Can we postpone the meeting?

to postpone
[to delay a meeting or an event]

I won't be at the meeting. Something unexpected has come up.

to come up
[to occur unexpectedly]

I'm afraid I have to cancel the team meeting on Friday.

to cancel
[to decide that a planned event will not happen]

Apologies, but I'm unable to attend due to other commitments.

to be unable to attend
[cannot go to]

23 Talking about your plans

One way of making plans with a co-worker or client is by using the present continuous to talk about what you are doing at the moment, or plans in the future.

⚙ **New language** The present continuous
Aa Vocabulary Making arrangements
🧩 **New skill** Talking about your plans

23.1 KEY LANGUAGE THE PRESENT CONTINUOUS

The present continuous is mostly used to describe ongoing events that are happening right now.

Are you busy at the moment?

Yes, I'm writing this report for Susan.

23.2 HOW TO FORM THE PRESENT CONTINUOUS

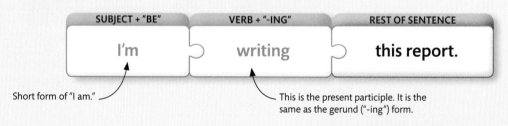

SUBJECT + "BE"	VERB + "-ING"	REST OF SENTENCE
I'm	writing	this report.

Short form of "I am."

This is the present participle. It is the same as the gerund ("-ing") form.

23.3 FURTHER EXAMPLES THE PRESENT CONTINUOUS

She's having **lunch downtown.**

They're having **a discussion.**

He is printing **the report.**

She is meeting **a new client.**

We are not enjoying **this meal.**

Add "not" after "be" to make the negative.

I'm not working **on my own.**

23.4 LISTEN TO THE AUDIO, THEN NUMBER THE PICTURES IN THE ORDER THEY ARE DESCRIBED

A ✓

B 1

C 2

D 4

E ☐

F 6

G 5

H 3

 23.5 FILL IN THE GAPS BY PUTTING THE VERBS IN THE PRESENT CONTINUOUS

The team _isn't having_ (not have) much success this year, so we _are trying_ (try) new things.

1 Sales _____ (increase) at the moment, so we _____ (get) a bigger bonus.

2 Fashions _____ (change), so we _____ (adapt) to new trends.

3 Travel costs _____ (rise) this year, so we _____ (call) each other more instead.

4 Profits _____ (drop), so we _____ (cut) costs in all areas of the business.

5 We _____ (sell) a lot to Asia, so we _____ (plan) to open an office there next year.

6 I can't believe you _____ (work) late. You _____ (miss) the staff party!

7 I _____ (wait) for my interview to start, and I _____ (feel) nervous.

8 The company _____ (lose) money, so we _____ (consider) a restructure.

🔊

23.6 KEY LANGUAGE QUESTIONS IN THE PRESENT CONTINUOUS

Questions in the present continuous can be formed by inverting the subject and "be," adding a question word for open questions.

To turn a statement into a question, swap the subject and "be."

Subject and "be" are inverted.

Who are we waiting for?

I'm not sure. Is James coming to this meeting?

Question words can be used before the verb to form open questions.

23.7 HOW TO FORM QUESTIONS IN THE PRESENT CONTINUOUS

QUESTION WORD	FORM OF "BE"	SUBJECT	VERB + "-ING"	REST OF SENTENCE
Who	**are**	**we**	**waiting**	**for?**

Using a question word like "where," "what," or "who" makes the question more open.

23.8 REWRITE THE SENTENCES, PUTTING THE WORDS IN THE CORRECT ORDER

| you | What | writing? | are |

What are you writing?

3. | we | selling | Are | that? |

Are we selling that?

1. | they | this? | Are | buying |

Are they buying this?

4. | him? | meeting | Are | you |

Are you meeting him?

2. | working | now? | it | Is |

Is it working now?

5. | promoting? | Who | they | are |

Who they are promoting?

88

23.9 MATCH THE QUESTIONS TO THE CORRECT ANSWERS

Where are you going?	Yes, I'm running two workshops.
❶ Why aren't they selling coffee?	He's giving a presentation.
❷ Who is giving this presentation?	I'm going to meet my new client.
❸ Are you doing any staff training?	No, I'm on the bus at the moment.
❹ What is Marco doing now?	That's Giorgio. He's a great speaker.
❺ Is he buying the company?	No, it's out of toner. I'm refilling it now.
❻ Are you taking the train home?	Yes, I think he is.
❼ Is the photocopier working?	There is no hot water left.

◀))

23.10 REWRITE THE STATEMENTS AS QUESTIONS IN THE PRESENT CONTINUOUS WITHOUT USING QUESTION WORDS

Mariam is working on the new project today.
Is Mariam working on the new project today?

❶ The company is buying everyone new laptops.

❷ Maria is giving her first presentation at the moment.

❸ Rakesh is designing the packaging for the new gadget.

❹ We are all going to the team meeting now.

❺ They are trying to improve sales in North America.

◀))

23.11 KEY LANGUAGE THE PRESENT CONTINUOUS FOR FUTURE ARRANGEMENTS

You can also use the present continuous to talk about fixed future plans. A clear date, day, or time is normally given.

I'm free next week. What are you doing **on Monday?**

This refers to fixed plans that have already been made.

I'm working **from home all day.**

Specific time reference is given.

23.12 MARK THE SENTENCES THAT ARE CORRECT

What are you doing on Monday? ☑
What are you doing on Mondays? ☐

1. I'm not coming to work tomorrow. ☐
   I not coming to work tomorrow. ☐

2. Are you meeting the team today? ☐
   Is you meeting the team today? ☐

3. I can't go. I'm not leaving until 8pm. ☐
   I can't go. I'm not leave until 8pm. ☐

4. Are we coming back here next year? ☐
   Will we coming back here next year? ☐

5. You are coming to the party later? ☐
   Are you coming to the party later? ☐

6. I'm not taking notes today. Are you? ☐
   I'm not take notes today. Are you? ☐

7. I'm having lunch at noon tomorrow. ☐
   I having lunch at noon tomorrow. ☐

8. Are you going to Asia this winter? ☐
   Will you going to Asia this winter? ☐

23.13 LISTEN TO THE AUDIO AND ANSWER THE QUESTIONS

Julia is calling a client, Jerome, to arrange a meeting.

Who is Julia trying to arrange a meeting for?
Julia and Jerome ☐
Jerome and Sylvie ☐
Jerome and Marie ☑

1. How long is Jerome staying in the city?
   Until Monday ☐
   For 10 days ☐
   He does not say ☐

2. When is Jerome taking Sylvie to the airport?
   Right now ☐
   Next Monday morning ☐
   Every Monday morning ☐

3. Where is the meeting taking place?
   In the bookstore ☐
   At the airport ☐
   In Marie's office ☐

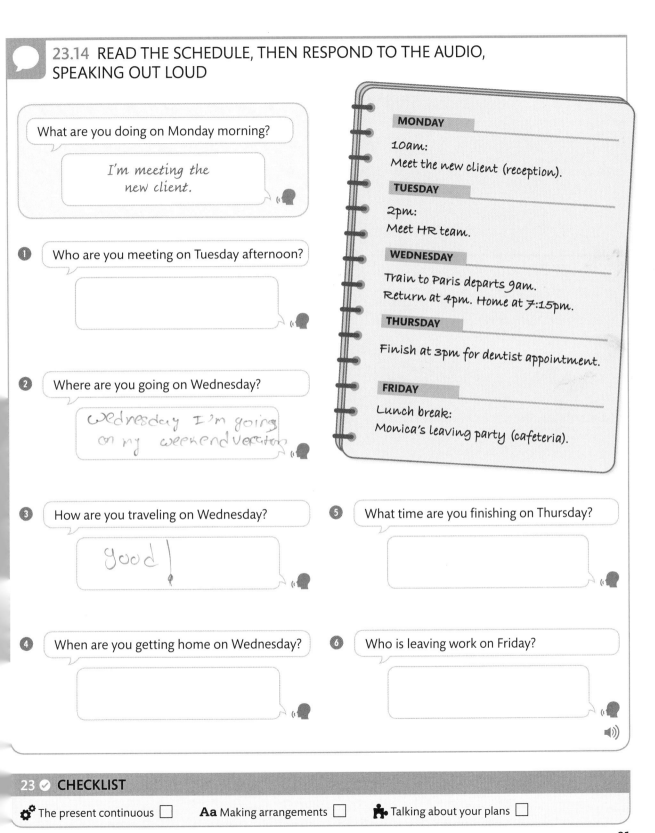

23.14 READ THE SCHEDULE, THEN RESPOND TO THE AUDIO, SPEAKING OUT LOUD

What are you doing on Monday morning?

> *I'm meeting the new client.*

MONDAY

10am:
Meet the new client (reception).

TUESDAY

2pm:
Meet HR team.

WEDNESDAY

Train to Paris departs 9am.
Return at 4pm. Home at 7:15pm.

THURSDAY

Finish at 3pm for dentist appointment.

FRIDAY

Lunch break:
Monica's leaving party (cafeteria).

① Who are you meeting on Tuesday afternoon?

② Where are you going on Wednesday?

> *Wednesday I'm going on my weekend vacation*

③ How are you traveling on Wednesday?

> *good!*

④ When are you getting home on Wednesday?

⑤ What time are you finishing on Thursday?

⑥ Who is leaving work on Friday?

---

24 Giving opinions

English speakers often use set phrases to signal that they want to interrupt without being rude. There are a number of ways to communicate your opinion politely.

⚙️ **New language** Interruptions and opinions
Aa Vocabulary Environmental issues
🧩 **New skill** Giving opinions politely

24.1 KEY LANGUAGE INTERRUPTING POLITELY

First, try to catch the speaker's eye or raise your hand. If you still do not get the chance to speak, starting your sentence with one of these phrases will help your interruption be polite.

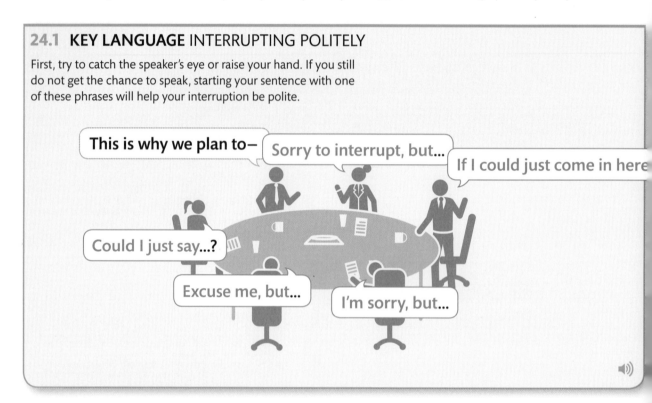

> This is why we plan to—

> Sorry to interrupt, but...

> If I could just come in here

> Could I just say...?

> Excuse me, but...

> I'm sorry, but...

🔊

24.2 MARK WHETHER EACH INTERRUPTION IS POLITE OR IMPOLITE

"Could I just say, this isn't the only option."
Polite ☑   **Impolite** ☐

❶ "What? I don't agree at all."
Polite ☐   **Impolite** ☐

❷ "I'm sorry, but I agree with Nick on this point."
Polite ☐   **Impolite** ☐

❸ "Excuse me, but I have some different figures."
Polite ☐   **Impolite** ☐

❹ "That's wrong and everyone knows it."
Polite ☐   **Impolite** ☐

❺ "Say that again. I don't believe it."
Polite ☐   **Impolite** ☐

❻ "If I could just come in here and mention losses."
Polite ☐   **Impolite** ☐

❼ "You don't know what you're talking about."
Polite ☐   **Impolite** ☐

🔊

24.3 KEY LANGUAGE EXCHANGING OPINIONS

It is also important to introduce your opinion respectfully, and it is polite to ask others for their thoughts.

You can soften your interruption by introducing your point politely.

In my opinion **we need to focus on recycling.**

What do you think?

Follow up your comments by asking others for their opinions.

24.4 FURTHER EXAMPLES EXCHANGING OPINIONS

I can see your point, but...

This structure can be followed by a noun or a gerund.

I'm not sure I agree. I think...

What do you think about **doing this?**

What do you think about **this idea?**

How about you?

24.5 RESPOND OUT LOUD TO THE AUDIO, FILLING IN THE GAPS USING THE WORDS IN THE PANEL

This is clearly the best approach.

I'm sorry, but I'm not sure I _____agree_____ .

1. We will lose thousands of customers.

   Sorry to _interrupt_, but my figures are different.

2. It's the same problem as last year.

   I'm not sure. What do you _think_ about new outlets?

3. These will never sell in Asia.

   I'm sorry, but in my _opinion_ they will sell well.

opinion

~~agree~~

interrupt

think

24.6 LISTEN TO THE AUDIO AND ANSWER THE QUESTIONS

The head of green policy at RonMax is holding a meeting to discuss the company's environmental strategy.

	True	False	Not given
The meeting is about past environmental policy.	☐	☐	✓
❶ RonMax currently recycles all its waste.	☐	☐	☐
❷ RonMax currently pays a company to take away waste paper.	☐	☐	☐
❸ Some rooms will not have lights on all the time.	☐	☐	☐
❹ Everyone agrees with the environmental strategy.	☐	☐	☐
❺ RonMax will publicly promote their green policies.	☐	☐	☐

Aa 24.7 READ THE ARTICLE, THEN COMPLETE THE COLLOCATIONS

attend / *schedule*	a meeting
❶	the minutes
❷	the agenda
❸	apologies
❹	vote
❺	remarks

ATTENDING AND SCHEDULING MEETINGS

During a meeting, someone takes "the minutes" (a record of what was said). You can review these afterward. Before a new meeting, you may be sent an outline ("the agenda"). Make sure to read this beforehand, and follow it as the meeting works through it. If you cannot go to a meeting, send your apologies. These will be announced at the meeting.

Sometimes the person in charge of the meeting ("the chair") takes a vote. He or she may have the casting vote if there is a tie. The best chairs keep the opening and closing remarks short.

Aa 24.8 READ THE CLUES AND WRITE THE ANSWERS IN THE CORRECT PLACES ON THE GRID

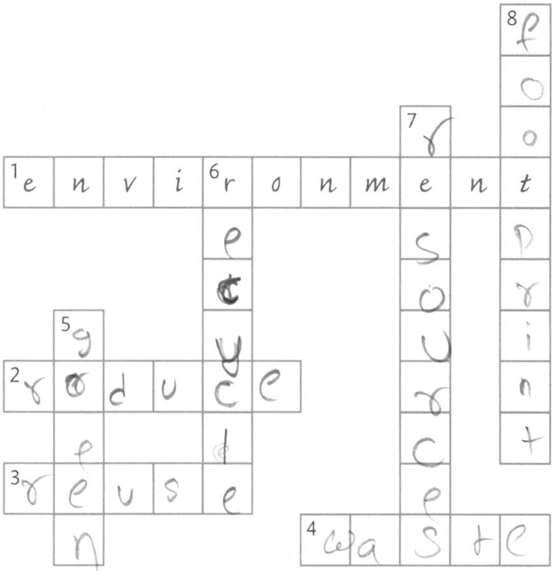

ACROSS

1. The air, water, and land around us all
2. Make an amount or number smaller
3. Use again
4. Something that is not used or wanted

DOWN

5. Environmentally friendly
6. Process something to make it usable again
7. Things that are available to be used
8. The mark or effect that something leaves behind

recycle ~~environment~~ green footprint reduce waste reuse resources

24.9 CROSS OUT THE INCORRECT WORD IN EACH SENTENCE

Can we ~~attend~~ / review the minutes?

1. Tim sent / said his apologies. He can't come.
2. Let's review our environmental / recycle strategy.
3. Let's work through the agenda / remarks quickly.
4. We should look at reducing / falling our waste.
5. I'm sorry to interrupt / disturb, but I disagree.
6. What do you think about / around recycling?
7. Let's make / take a vote on the new policy.
8. The meeting chair has the casting / chasing vote.
9. I'm sorry / apologize, but I don't agree.
10. I think it's the best strategy. How about / do you?
11. I just have a few closed / closing remarks.

24 CHECKLIST

Interruptions and opinions ☐ Aa Environmental issues ☐ Giving opinions politely ☐

25 Agreeing and disagreeing

When you react to someone's opinion, it is important to be polite and respectful. This is especially important when you disagree with someone.

⚙ **New language** Reacting to opinions
Aa Vocabulary Agreeing and disagreeing
🧩 **New skill** Discussing opinions

25.1 KEY LANGUAGE AGREEING WITH AN OPINION

There are many ways to say that you agree with someone. You do not need to say very much and, sometimes, people just nod.

STRONG AGREEMENT

We need to focus on sales this quarter.

Exactly.

Absolutely.

That's a good point.

Yes, I agree.

WEAK AGREEMENT

These interns have been a huge help.

I suppose so.

I suppose you're right.

The language of agreement changes according to whether you are agreeing with a positive or a negative statement.

AGREEING WITH A POSITIVE STATEMENT

I think our system needs updating.

Me too.

So do I.

AGREEING WITH A NEGATIVE STATEMENT

I don't like the new office at all.

Me neither.

Nor do I.

25.2 MARK THE BEST REPLY TO EACH STATEMENT

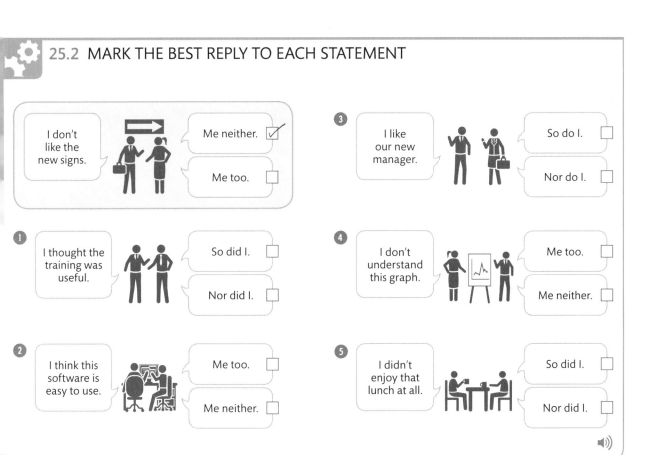

I don't like the new signs.
- Me neither. ✓
- Me too. ☐

❸ I like our new manager.
- So do I. ☐
- Nor do I. ☐

❶ I thought the training was useful.
- So did I. ☐
- Nor did I. ☐

❹ I don't understand this graph.
- Me too. ☐
- Me neither. ☐

❷ I think this software is easy to use.
- Me too. ☐
- Me neither. ☐

❺ I didn't enjoy that lunch at all.
- So did I. ☐
- Nor did I. ☐

25.3 MATCH THE STATEMENTS TO THE RESPONSES

I think the new Marketing team is great! → Me too. They're very hardworking.

❶ I thought the talk was really interesting.

❷ I didn't understand that complicated talk.

❸ The new head of admin is very efficient.

❹ It's good that we can buy parking permits.

❺ I like the new packaging designs.

❻ I didn't like the old head of HR.

❼ I thought the lunch was great today.

Nor did I. It was too difficult.

Me too. They're practical and cheap.

Me too. They're very hardworking.

Neither did I. He was always moody.

Yes, I agree. She is very friendly, too.

So did I. The menu was excellent.

I suppose so, but they are expensive.

I suppose you're right, but it was so long!

25.4 KEY LANGUAGE DISAGREEING WITH AN OPINION

English speakers often use a variety of polite phrases to express degrees of disagreement.

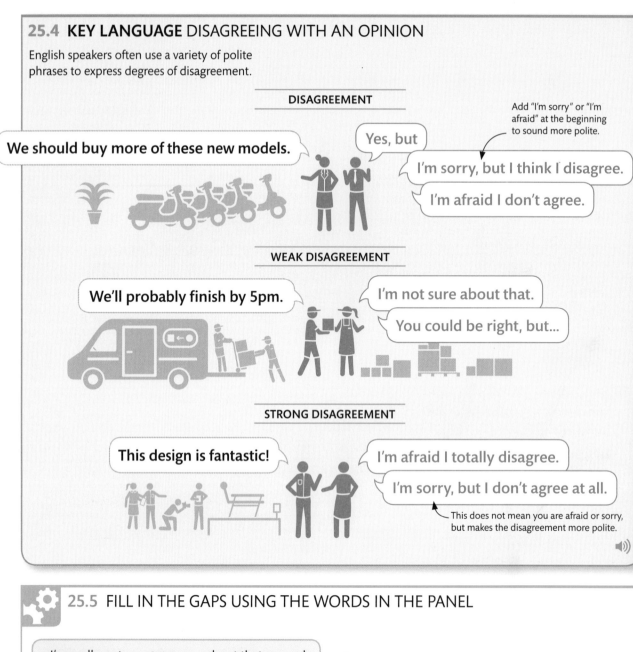

DISAGREEMENT

We should buy more of these new models.

Yes, but

Add "I'm sorry" or "I'm afraid" at the beginning to sound more polite.

I'm sorry, but I think I disagree.

I'm afraid I don't agree.

WEAK DISAGREEMENT

We'll probably finish by 5pm.

I'm not sure about that.

You could be right, but...

STRONG DISAGREEMENT

This design is fantastic!

I'm afraid I totally disagree.

I'm sorry, but I don't agree at all.

This does not mean you are afraid or sorry, but makes the disagreement more polite.

25.5 FILL IN THE GAPS USING THE WORDS IN THE PANEL

I'm really not ___sure___ about that new ad.

① You could be __right__ , but I think it's ugly.

② I'm _____ we disagree about the price.

③ I'm _____ , but I don't agree, Jan.

④ I'm afraid I _____ . It's too expensive.

⑤ I'm sorry, Joe, but I don't agree _____ all.

| sorry | right | sure | at | disagree | afraid |

98

25.6 LISTEN TO THE AUDIO AND ANSWER THE QUESTIONS

Jeremy and Sian are discussing recent proposals for change in their workplace.

What does Jeremy think about the changes?

He likes all of them ☐
He likes some of them ☑
He dislikes all of them ☐

① Sian loves the idea of shower rooms.

Jeremy strongly agrees with her ☐
Jeremy agrees with her ☐
Jeremy strongly disagrees with her ☐

② Sian is looking forward to a choice of coffees.

Jeremy strongly agrees with her ☐
Jeremy agrees with her ☐
Jeremy strongly disagrees with her ☐

③ Jeremy liked having meetings on Mondays.

Sian strongly agrees with him ☐
Sian agrees with him ☐
Sian disagrees with him ☐

④ Sian is looking forward to the convention in Santiago.

Jeremy strongly agrees with her ☐
Jeremy agrees with her ☐
Jeremy strongly disagrees with her ☐

25.7 CROSS OUT THE INCORRECT WORD IN EACH SENTENCE, THEN SAY THE SENTENCES OUT LOUD

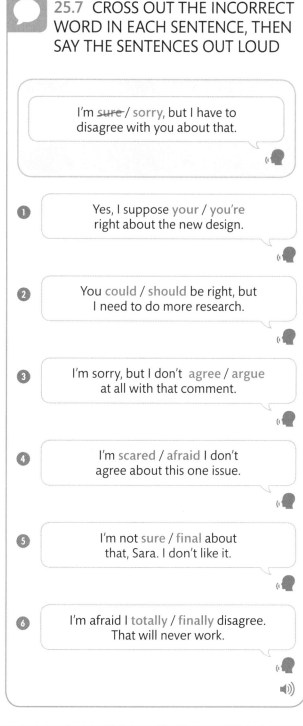

I'm ~~sure~~ / sorry, but I have to disagree with you about that.

① Yes, I suppose your / you're right about the new design.

② You could / should be right, but I need to do more research.

③ I'm sorry, but I don't agree / argue at all with that comment.

④ I'm scared / afraid I don't agree about this one issue.

⑤ I'm not sure / final about that, Sara. I don't like it.

⑥ I'm afraid I totally / finally disagree. That will never work.

---

25 ✓ CHECKLIST

⚙ Reacting to opinions ☐   **Aa** Agreeing and disagreeing ☐   🧩 Discussing opinions ☐

26 Health and safety

Many workplaces issue guidelines for how to avoid accidents and stay safe. In English, this topic often uses specialist vocabulary and reflexive pronouns.

⚙ **New language** Reflexive pronouns
Aa Vocabulary Health and safety at work
🧩 **New skill** Talking about safety at work

26.1 KEY LANGUAGE REFLEXIVE PRONOUNS

Reflexive pronouns show that the subject of a verb is the same as its object.

The subject pronoun refers to the person doing the action.

Follow the guidelines so you don't hurt yourself.

Use a reflexive pronoun when the subject and object of a sentence are the same.

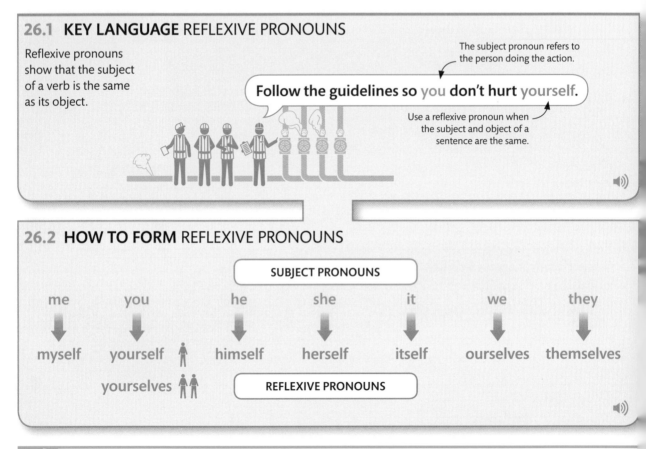

26.2 HOW TO FORM REFLEXIVE PRONOUNS

SUBJECT PRONOUNS

me	you	he	she	it	we	they
↓	↓	↓	↓	↓	↓	↓
myself	yourself	himself	herself	itself	ourselves	themselves
	yourselves					

REFLEXIVE PRONOUNS

 ## 26.3 MARK WHICH SENTENCES ARE CORRECT

She cut herself on the machinery. ☑
She cut itself on the machinery. ☐

1️⃣ They locked themselves in the fridge. ☐
They locked themselfs in the fridge. ☐

2️⃣ He burned himself on the coffee machine. ☐
He burned herself on the coffee machine. ☐

3️⃣ Both of you, protect yourself from the sun. ☐
Both of you, protect yourselves from the sun. ☐

4️⃣ We booked ourself on a fire safety course. ☐
We booked ourselves on a fire safety course. ☐

5️⃣ I fell and hurt myself on the wet floor. ☐
I fell and hurt yourself on the wet floor. ☐

26.4 READ THE ARTICLE AND ANSWER THE QUESTIONS

The author is surprised that accidents happen at work.
True ☐ **False** ☐ **Not given** ☑

1. The author hurt himself at work last year.
True ☐ **False** ☐ **Not given** ☐

2. The author does not think health and safety regulations are important.
True ☐ **False** ☐ **Not given** ☐

3. You should tell your employer if you have an accident at work.
True ☐ **False** ☐ **Not given** ☐

Protect yourself at work

How to prevent accidents in the workplace

We spend a lot of our time at work, so it is not surprising that we have accidents there. But what can you do to protect yourself and help your co-workers protect themselves from injury? The first thing is to make sure that your company follows all the sensible health and safety regulations. Most accidents are caused by slips, trips, lifting, and carrying. If you do hurt yourself at work, report it to your employer and don't blame yourself. You could ask to take a first aid course so that you can protect and, if necessary, treat yourself and your co-workers.

Aa 26.5 MATCH THE PICTURES TO THE CORRECT PHRASES

fire exit

fire alarm

fire extinguisher

assembly point

first aid kit

🔊

26.6 CROSS OUT THE INCORRECT WORDS IN EACH SENTENCE, THEN SAY THE SENTENCES OUT LOUD

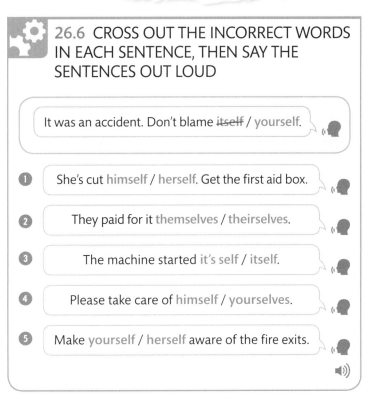

It was an accident. Don't blame ~~itself~~ / yourself. 🗣

1. She's cut himself / herself. Get the first aid box. 🗣

2. They paid for it themselves / theirselves. 🗣

3. The machine started it's self / itself. 🗣

4. Please take care of himself / yourselves. 🗣

5. Make yourself / herself aware of the fire exits. 🗣

🔊

26 ✓ CHECKLIST

⚙ Reflexive pronouns ☐   **Aa** Health and safety at work ☐   🧩 Talking about safety at work ☐

27 Suggestions and advice

When there are everyday problems in the workplace, it is useful to know how to make suggestions and offer advice. There are several ways to do this in English.

⚙ **New language** Prefixes and suffixes
Aa Vocabulary Everyday workplace problems
🧩 **New skill** Making suggestions

27.1 KEY LANGUAGE MAKING SUGGESTIONS

You can use a number of phrases to offer advice or make suggestions.
Some of these take the base form of the verb, and others need the "-ing" form.

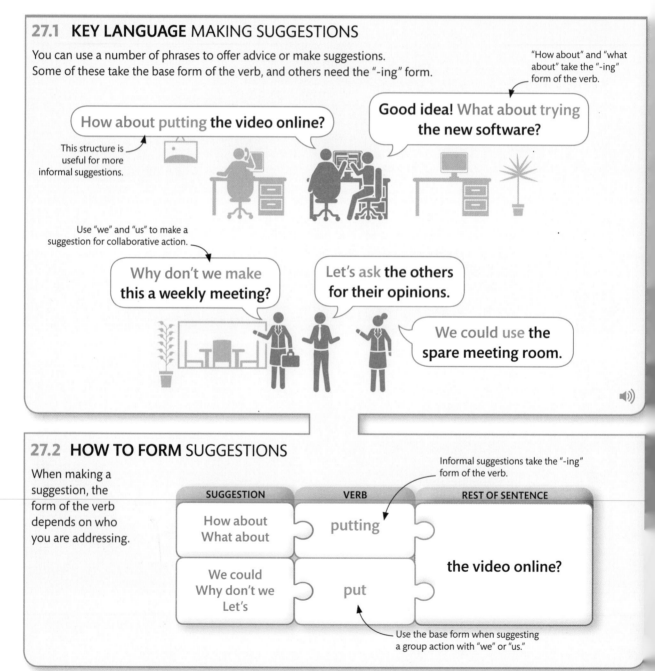

"How about" and "what about" take the "-ing" form of the verb.

How about putting **the video online?**

This structure is useful for more informal suggestions.

Good idea! What about trying **the new software?**

Use "we" and "us" to make a suggestion for collaborative action.

Why don't we make **this a weekly meeting?**

Let's ask **the others for their opinions.**

We could use **the spare meeting room.**

27.2 HOW TO FORM SUGGESTIONS

When making a suggestion, the form of the verb depends on who you are addressing.

Informal suggestions take the "-ing" form of the verb.

SUGGESTION	VERB	REST OF SENTENCE
How about / What about	putting	the video online?
We could / Why don't we / Let's	put	

Use the base form when suggesting a group action with "we" or "us."

27.3 REWRITE THE SENTENCES, PUTTING THE WORDS IN THE CORRECT ORDER

| building | new | about | a | How | website? |

How about building a new website?

① | Let's | more | media. | on | do | promotion | social |

_____

② | could | the | product. | We | redesign | packaging | this | for |

_____

③ | about | a | consultant? | software | What | hiring |

_____

◀))

27.4 KEY LANGUAGE OFFERING ADVICE WITH "SHOULD" + BASE FORM

One way to offer stronger advice is using "should" or "shouldn't," which suggests negative consequences if ignored.

You should try to keep the meeting short.

— Base form of main verb

◀))

27.5 MATCH THE WORKPLACE PROBLEMS TO THE SUGGESTIONS AND ADVICE

| The printer is broken. | → | You should reset the router. |

① The internet is down again. — I should order some more.

② Sara scraped the director's car. — We should call an engineer.

③ There's only one package of coffee left. — She should tell him before he sees it.

④ The fridge door has been open all day. — He should walk around the office.

⑤ Jeremy sits at the computer all day. — We should throw away the food.

◀))

27.6 KEY LANGUAGE CHANGING MEANING WITH PREFIXES AND SUFFIXES

Prefixes and suffixes change the meaning of words that they are added to.
Sometimes this also changes the word's form (such as from a noun to an adjective).

 **careful**   **careless**

Adding "-ful" to a noun forms
an adjective with a sense of
"full of" that noun.

Adding "-less" to a noun forms an
adjective meaning "not having"
or "not affected by" that noun.

There are several
prefixes that can
be used to form
a new word with the
opposite meaning.

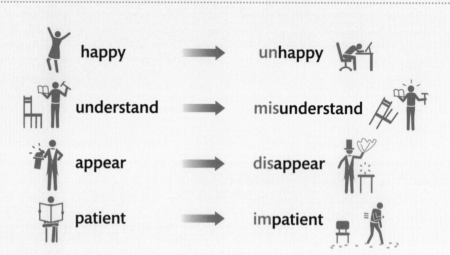

happy ➡ **unhappy**

understand ➡ **misunderstand**

appear ➡ **disappear**

patient ➡ **impatient**

 ## 27.7 FILL IN THE GAPS USING THE WORDS IN THE PANEL

This time slot is ___*impractical*___ . Why don't we rearrange it?

❶ I am _____ to come in the morning. How about the afternoon?

❷ I _____ words so often. Why don't we get an editor?

❸ The machine isn't working. We should _____ it.

❹ Are you _____ ? Why don't we call a doctor for you?

❺ These tests are _____ . What about doing easier ones?

impossible
~~impractical~~
unable
disconnect
misspell
unwell

27.8 LISTEN TO THE AUDIO, THEN NUMBER THE PICTURES IN THE ORDER THEY ARE DESCRIBED

 B 1
 C ☐
D ☐
E ☐

27.9 CROSS OUT THE INCORRECT WORD IN EACH SENTENCE, THEN SAY THE SENTENCES OUT LOUD

Why don't we keep notes so we don't **misunderstand** / ~~understand~~ the plan?

❶ Let's use our old system again. This new one is so **familiar** / **unfamiliar** and slow.

❷ How about changing the time so that more people are **able** / **unable** to come.

❸ Let's discuss the negative feedback from people who **agree** / **disagree** with our plan.

❹ What about explaining the delay to stop people from becoming so **impatient** / **patient**.

❺ I love conventions! It's so easy to **connect** / **disconnect** with new people.

❻ I have no idea how to write this report. It seems **possible** / **impossible**!

27 ✓ CHECKLIST

⚙ Prefixes and suffixes ☐   **Aa** Everyday workplace problems ☐   🧩 Making suggestions ☐

28 Giving a presentation

When you are preparing a presentation, make sure it is clear and easy to follow. There are certain phrases you can use to help guide the audience through the talk.

⚙️ **New language** Signposting language
Aa Vocabulary Presentation equipment
🧩 **New skill** Structuring a talk

28.1 KEY LANGUAGE BEGINNING A PRESENTATION

If you outline the structure of your presentation at the start, it makes it easier for the audience to follow what you are saying. Signposting language can help you to do this effectively.

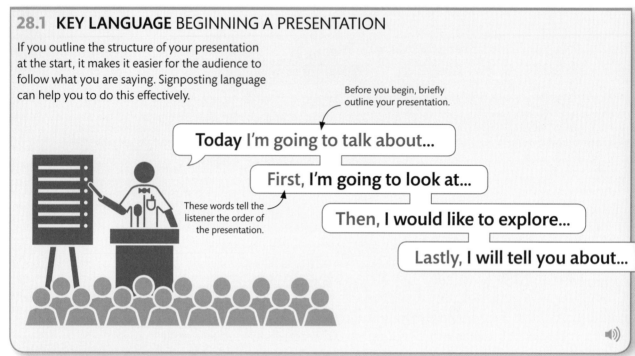

Before you begin, briefly outline your presentation.

Today I'm going to talk about...

First, I'm going to look at...

These words tell the listener the order of the presentation.

Then, I would like to explore...

Lastly, I will tell you about...

28.2 FILL IN THE GAPS USING THE PHRASES IN THE PANEL

Today I'm going to ___talk about___ a new approach that we want to try.

1 To _____ this talk I will give an overall introduction to the project.

2 _____ , after the introduction, I'll describe our role in the project.

3 Next, we'll _____ the benefits of this approach.

4 After _____ , we'll look at the possible difficulties we might have.

5 Then, to _____ , we'll look at what future research we can do.

6 Lastly, I will _____ any questions that you have for me.

answer
finish
Second
explore
~~talk about~~
that
start

28.3 KEY LANGUAGE CHANGING TOPICS

You can also use signposting language to move between topics during your presentation.

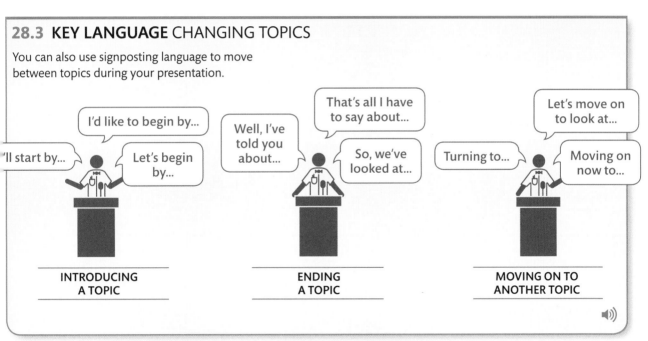

I'd like to begin by...

'll start by...

Let's begin by...

INTRODUCING A TOPIC

Well, I've told you about...

That's all I have to say about...

So, we've looked at...

ENDING A TOPIC

Turning to...

Let's move on to look at...

Moving on now to...

MOVING ON TO ANOTHER TOPIC

28.4 LISTEN TO THE AUDIO AND ANSWER THE QUESTIONS

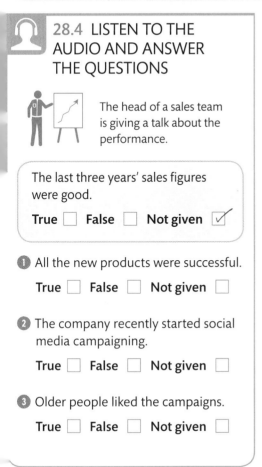

The head of a sales team is giving a talk about the performance.

The last three years' sales figures were good.

True ☐ **False** ☐ **Not given** ☑

❶ All the new products were successful.

True ☐ **False** ☐ **Not given** ☐

❷ The company recently started social media campaigning.

True ☐ **False** ☐ **Not given** ☐

❸ Older people liked the campaigns.

True ☐ **False** ☐ **Not given** ☐

Aa 28.5 MATCH THE DEFINITIONS TO THE PRESENTATION EQUIPMENT

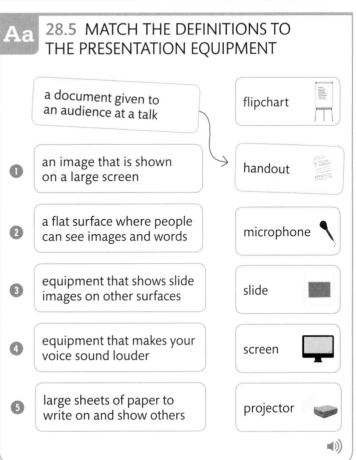

a document given to an audience at a talk → flipchart

❶ an image that is shown on a large screen → handout

❷ a flat surface where people can see images and words — microphone

❸ equipment that shows slide images on other surfaces — slide

❹ equipment that makes your voice sound louder — screen

❺ large sheets of paper to write on and show others — projector

28.6 KEY LANGUAGE ENDING A PRESENTATION

At the end of your presentation, you can give a brief summary of your points and, if you want, allow the audience to ask questions.

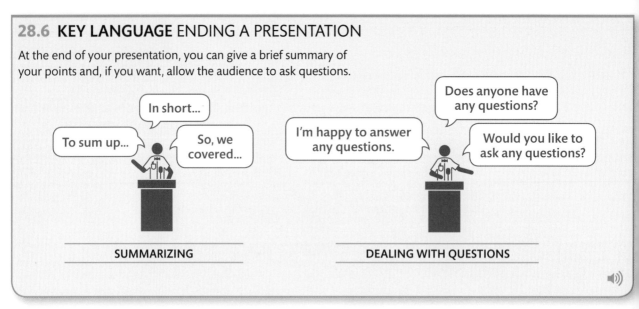

To sum up...

In short...

So, we covered...

SUMMARIZING

I'm happy to answer any questions.

Does anyone have any questions?

Would you like to ask any questions?

DEALING WITH QUESTIONS

28.7 REWRITE THE SENTENCES, PUTTING THE WORDS IN THE CORRECT ORDER

a | sum | is | To | big | year. | up, | this

To sum up, this is a big year.

1 happy | questions. | I'm | answer | to | any

_____

2 we've | main | So, | covered | the | issues.

_____

3 have | anyone | Does | questions? | any

_____

4 to | anything? | you | Would | like | ask

_____

5 next | important. | In | short, | is | year

_____

28.8 LISTEN TO THE AUDIO, THEN NUMBER THE SENTENCES IN THE ORDER YOU HEAR THEM

A company's head of marketing is talking about their new range.

Ⓐ That's all I have to say about the product. ☐

Ⓑ Does anyone have anything they want to ask? ☐

Ⓒ Let's move on to look at the promotion materials. ☐

Ⓓ I'd like to begin by showing you something new. ☐

Ⓔ So, we briefly covered the product, and the promotion. ☐

Ⓕ Today I'm going to talk about our new range of products. ☐ 1

Ⓖ I'm happy to answer any questions you may have. ☐

28.9 CROSS OUT THE INCORRECT WORD IN EACH SENTENCE, THEN SAY THE SENTENCES OUT LOUD

To / ~~For~~ start, let's look at the way the company has performed.

1. In **tall** / **short** we are very proud of our new products.

2. I'd like to **beginning** / **begin** by looking back at past sales.

3. That's all I have to **say** / **talk** about the advertising campaign.

4. Let's move **up** / **on** to talk about the packaging we've designed.

5. Does anyone **have** / **make** any questions for me?

---

28 ⊘ CHECKLIST

⚙ Signposting language ☐   **Aa** Presentations and talks ☐   🧩 Structuring a talk ☐

↻ REVIEW THE ENGLISH YOU HAVE LEARNED IN UNITS 22–28

NEW LANGUAGE	SAMPLE SENTENCE	☑	UNIT
THE PRESENT CONTINUOUS FOR ONGOING EVENTS AND FUTURE PLANS	I'm finishing **this report.** I'm working **from home on Monday.**	☐	23.1, 23.6, 23.11
INTERRUPTING POLITELY AND EXCHANGING OPINIONS	Sorry to interrupt, but... I'm not sure I agree... How about you?	☐	24.1, 24.3
AGREEING AND DISAGREEING	I suppose you're right... I'm afraid I totally disagree.	☐	25.1, 25.4
REFLEXIVE PRONOUNS	Follow the guidelines so you **don't hurt** yourself.	☐	26.1
MAKING SUGGESTIONS AND GIVING ADVICE	How about putting **the video online?** You should try **to keep the meeting short.**	☐	27.1, 27.4
SIGNPOSTING LANGUAGE FOR PRESENTATIONS	First, **I'm going to look at...**	☐	28.1, 28.3, 28.6

29 Rules and requests

Use "can" and "have to" to talk about rules in the workplace, and verbs such as "could" to politely ask colleagues to help you solve problems.

⚙ **New language** Modal verbs
Aa Vocabulary Polite requests
🧩 **New skill** Talking about rules and regulations

29.1 KEY LANGUAGE MODAL VERBS FOR PERMISSION

Use "can" to give a colleague permission to do something.

> You can take your lunch break at 1 o'clock.

Use "can't" to say that a colleague is not allowed to do something.

> There's a business dress code here. You can't wear shorts to work.

"Have to" expresses a strong obligation to do something.

> That's the fire alarm! We have to leave the store now.

"Don't have to" means that something is not necessary.

> You don't have to stay late tonight. We're not very busy.

🔊

⚙ 29.2 MATCH THE PAIRS OF SENTENCES THAT GO TOGETHER

You can listen to music at work.	It's a special one for fire safety.
❶ You have to close that door.	We're meeting clients later this afternoon.
❷ You don't have to eat at your desk.	Just make sure it's not too loud.
❸ You can't leave early today.	I have saved all the documents.
❹ You can shut the computers down.	There's a nice café across the street.

🔊

29.3 FILL IN THE GAPS USING THE WORDS IN THE PANEL

You _____can't_____ park your car there. It's the CEO's space.

1 Is your stapler broken? You _____ use mine.

2 She _____ come to the training session. She did it last year.

3 You _____ turn off the light if you're the last person to leave the office.

4 He _____ test the fire alarm every Wednesday morning.

5 We _____ wear a jacket and tie to work in the summer months.

can't   have to   has to   don't have to   can   doesn't have to

29.4 READ THE NOTICE AND ANSWER THE QUESTIONS

All staff are allowed to wear jeans to work.
True ☐ **False** ☐ **Not given** ☑

1 Staff get free breakfast at the restaurant.
True ☐ **False** ☐ **Not given** ☐

2 All staff must have short hair.
True ☐ **False** ☐ **Not given** ☐

3 Staff are allowed to keep tips from the clients.
True ☐ **False** ☐ **Not given** ☐

4 Staff are not allowed to leave the kitchen dirty.
True ☐ **False** ☐ **Not given** ☐

5 Staff only wash their hands after touching food.
True ☐ **False** ☐ **Not given** ☐

KITCHEN RULES:

- Kitchen staff can wear jeans and sneakers
- Waiting staff have to wear uniform at all times
- All staff can drink free tea, coffee, and soft drinks
- You have to keep cell phones in your locker
- You don't have to cut your hair, but do tie it back
- You don't have to pay for lunch or dinner
- You can keep any tips given by customers
- You can't use bad language in the restaurant
- You have to clean the kitchen before you leave
- And remember that you have to wash your hands before and after touching food

29.5 KEY LANGUAGE POLITE REQUESTS WITH MODAL VERBS

Use "Could you" with a base verb, or "Would you mind" with a gerund, to politely ask for help with problems at work.

TIP
Business English rarely uses negative forms of these requests because they are less polite than the positive forms.

We've run out of hangers. {
Could you order
Would you mind ordering
} **some more?**

29.6 HOW TO FORM POLITE REQUESTS WITH MODAL VERBS

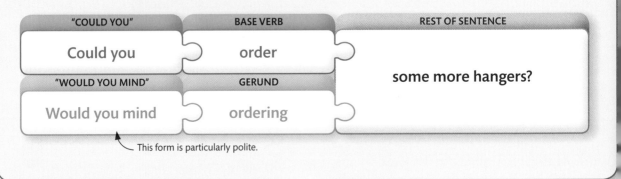

"COULD YOU"	BASE VERB	REST OF SENTENCE
Could you	order	
"WOULD YOU MIND"	**GERUND**	some more hangers?
Would you mind	ordering	

This form is particularly polite.

29.7 FURTHER EXAMPLES POLITE REQUESTS WITH MODAL VERBS

This box is really heavy. Could you help **me lift it?**

I can't find my stapler. Could you lend **me yours, please?**

You can add "please" to make requests more polite.

The clients are here early. Would you mind making **them tea and coffee?**

Our card machine isn't **working.** Would you mind paying **with cash?**

29.8 CROSS OUT THE INCORRECT WORD IN EACH SENTENCE

Would you mind ~~close~~ / closing the door?

1 Could you **tell** / telling Jan to call me back?

2 Could you checking / **check** this report?

3 Would you mind ordering / **order** more pens?

4 Could you **mop** / mopping the floor, please?

5 Could you coming / **come** to today's meeting?

6 Would you mind calling / **call** back later?

7 Would you mind turning / **turn** the light off?

8 Could you **wash** / washing these cups, please?

9 Could you passing / **pass** around the reports?

10 Would you mind **book** / booking me a taxi?

11 Could you showing / **show** our clients around?

◀))

29.9 LISTEN TO THE AUDIO AND ANSWER THE QUESTIONS

Robin is asking a co-worker, Bruno, to help him prepare for a difficult meeting with their suppliers.

Bruno has finished his presentation.
True ☑ **False** ☐

1 Robin doesn't need help with his handout.
True ☐ **False** ☐

2 The suppliers are a new company.
True ☐ **False** ☐

3 Bruno will check Robin's handouts.
True ☐ **False** ☐

4 Robin asks Bruno to call the taxi company.
True ☐ **False** ☐

29.10 USE THE CHART TO CREATE SIX CORRECT SENTENCES AND SAY THEM OUT LOUD

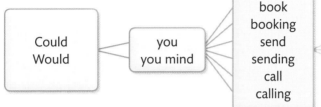

Could you book a meeting room?

| Could / Would | you / you mind | book / booking / send / sending / call / calling | a meeting room? / Sam Davies an email? / our supplier? |

◀))

29 ✓ CHECKLIST

⚙ Modal verbs ☐   **Aa** Polite requests ☐   🧩 Talking about rules and regulations ☐

113

30 Vocabulary

30.1 WORK IDIOMS

The road is closed, but it's business as usual in the store.

business as usual
[the normal daily routine at a company]

Spending any more on that useless product would be throwing money down the drain.

throwing money down the drain
[wasting money]

There's so much red tape involved in importing food products.

red tape
[administration, paperwork, or rules and regulations]

You get a free car and the company gets good press. It's a win-win situation.

a win-win situation
[a situation with no negative outcome]

Our sales were poor this year and we're in the red.

to be in the red
[to owe money]

They have to work around the clock to redecorate the shop.

to work around the clock
[to work very long hours]

I can't come home yet, I'm snowed under with work.

to be snowed under
[to have too much work to do]

Sorry, he can't come to the phone. He's tied up with another client.

to be tied up with
[to be busy doing something else]

I hope I can wind down a bit over the weekend.

to wind down
[to gradually relax]

Take it easy! We've got another hour to finish decorating the conference hall.

to take it easy
[to relax or calm down]

Sorry, I'll have to miss lunch. I'm swamped with invoices to file.

to be swamped
[to be really busy]

I hate being on the top floor when the elevator is out of order.

to be out of order
[to not be working]

She's not a great team member. She doesn't really pull her weight.

to pull your weight
[to do a fair share of work]

We've told you our final price. The ball is in your court now.

the ball is in your court
[it is your turn to do or say something]

This report is due today. I can't put it off any longer.

to put something off
[to delay or avoid something]

Greg is really creative and often thinks outside the box.

to think outside the box
[to think about a something in an original way]

They are very difficult clients because they're always moving the goalposts.

to move the goalposts
[to change the desired end result]

If we're all here, Marcia, can you get the ball rolling?

to get the ball rolling
[to start something]

I don't understand all these error messages. My laptop's going haywire!

going haywire
[not acting or behaving as it should]

I want to finish by five o'clock, so let's get down to business.

to get down to business
[to start work on something that needs doing]

115

31 Discussing issues

Many common workplace problems arise from an ongoing situation in the past. You can use the past continuous tense to discuss these problems.

🔧 **New language** Past continuous
Aa Vocabulary Work idioms
🧩 **New skill** Describing workplace problems

31.1 KEY LANGUAGE THE PAST CONTINUOUS

Use the past continuous to describe problems or situations that were ongoing in the past, but are now finished.

The action started in the past and continued for some time.

This morning was awful. My managers were complaining **about my work**

PAST   NOW

31.2 FURTHER EXAMPLES THE PAST CONTINUOUS

The coffee machine wasn't working **this morning. Is it fixed now?**

Were **you** taking **notes in that meetin I can't remember what we have to d**

PAST   NOW

PAST   NOW

31.3 HOW TO FORM THE PAST CONTINUOUS

SUBJECT	"WAS / WERE"	VERB + "-ING"	REST OF SENTENCE
My managers	were	complaining	about my work.

Use "was" or "were" depending on the subject.

Add "-ing" to the main verb.

31.4 FILL IN THE GAPS BY PUTTING THE VERBS IN THE PAST CONTINUOUS

Angel _____was writing_____ (write) his report this morning. He still hasn't finished.

1 Gabino _____ (not listen) during the team meeting this morning.

2 The internet _____ (not work) all day yesterday. I had to call my clients.

3 Hannah and Luke _____ (talk) during the CEO's presentation.

4 I _____ (forget) to do everyday jobs, so I wrote a list.

5 I put you on a new team because you _____ (lose) sales.

🔊

31.5 READ THE ARTICLE AND WRITE ANSWERS TO THE QUESTIONS AS FULL SENTENCES

R CAREER

our problems solved

experts are here to help solve your workplace problems

ast week I was reading all your emails about problems with co-workers. Most of us know meone in the office who can be a little bit lazy metimes, but Maria wrote last week to say that r co-worker was not answering important ails and leaving Maria to reply to all the sales quiries. Well, my advice, Maria, is to talk to your -worker first. Perhaps he was going through a fficult time. I know it is difficult if your co-worker also your friend, but you must make sure at you don't end up doing your work and his as well!

Remember José from last onth, who was feeling ery tired after lunch every ay? Well, he did change is diet so that he ate more alads and vegetables and aid last week that he was vorking until 5pm every lay without feeling exhausted. Great news, José!

A healthy lunch will give you more energy at work

What was the author doing last week?

The author was reading emails.

1 What wasn't Maria's co-worker doing?

_____

2 What was he leaving Maria to do?

_____

3 What was the author's advice?

_____

4 What was José's problem last month?

_____

5 What did he do to solve the problem?

_____

6 How late was José working last week?

_____

31.6 LISTEN TO THE AUDIO, THEN NUMBER THE PICTURES IN THE ORDER THEY ARE DESCRIBED

A

B 1

C

D

E

Aa 31.7 REWRITE THE SENTENCES, CORRECTING THE ERRORS

I was **working about** the clock today
I was working around the clock today.

1 Sales were improving. It was **win-win** situation.

_____

2 It's a difficult task. We must think **out** the box.

_____

3 The team was throwing money **up** the drain.

_____

4 Was your assistant **pushing** his weight today?

_____

5 We were working with a lot of **blue** tape.

_____

6 Now we're all here, let's get **in** to business.

_____

Aa 31.8 MATCH THE PICTURES TO THE CORRECT SENTENCES

The printer was going haywire yesterday.

1

I kept putting off a difficult phone call this morning.

2

The elevator is out of order.

3

I'm tied up with these difficult reports.

4

Our sales fell last year. Now we're in the red.

31.9 READ THE EMAIL THEN ANSWER THE QUESTIONS, SPEAKING OUT LOUD

✉   ✕ ⌄

To: Faruk

Subject: Work stress

Hi Faruk,

It's great to hear from you. I am still working around the clock on the project we were talking about. I am trying to design the packaging for the new health tracker watch, but time's running out. Every time I show the marketing department a design, people send me so many new emails that I feel snowed under. I'm so up to my ears with silly emails that I can't do any real work for the project. This means even though I'm always on the go, I don't seem to get much work done. My husband, Mark, says that I should take it easy because I'm quite stressed and miserable at home too, but I find it hard to wind down on weekends. I know you've worked in marketing for a long time, and just wondered if you have any advice for me?

Thanks so much, Gloria

↩ ↩↩   ■ 📎 ⌐

What does Gloria say about her workload?

She is working around the clock

3 Why doesn't Gloria get much work done?

1 What project is Gloria working on?

4 What does Mark want Gloria to do?

2 Who sends Gloria lots of emails?

5 Why has Gloria written to Faruk?

◀))

---

31 ✓ CHECKLIST

⚙ Past continuous ☐   **Aa** Work idioms ☐   🤝 Describing workplace problems ☐

32 Apologies and explanations

English uses a variety of polite phrases to apologize for mistakes. Use the past continuous with the past simple to offer an explanation for a mistake.

⚙ **New language** Past continuous and past simple
Aa Vocabulary Workplace mistakes
🧩 **New skill** Apologizing and giving explanations

32.1 KEY LANGUAGE APOLOGIES AND RESPONSES

There are many formal and informal phrases that you can use to make and respond to apologies. Responses can either accept the apology to end the conversation, or reject it to ask for further action.

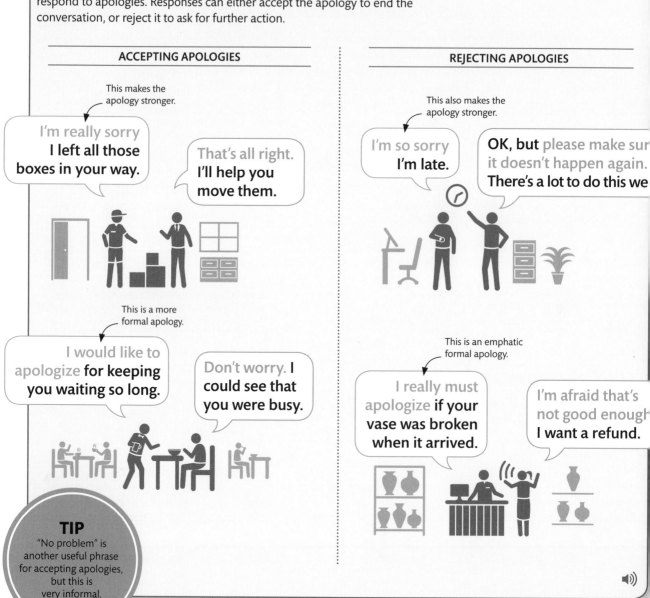

ACCEPTING APOLOGIES

This makes the apology stronger.

I'm really sorry **I left all those boxes in your way.**

That's all right. **I'll help you move them.**

This is a more formal apology.

I would like to apologize **for keeping you waiting so long.**

Don't worry. I **could see that you were busy.**

REJECTING APOLOGIES

This also makes the apology stronger.

I'm so sorry **I'm late.**

OK, but please make sur[e] it doesn't happen again. **There's a lot to do this we[ek]**

This is an emphatic formal apology.

I really must apologize **if your vase was broken when it arrived.**

I'm afraid that's not good enoug[h] **I want a refund.**

TIP
"No problem" is another useful phrase for accepting apologies, but this is very informal.

32.2 MATCH THE APOLOGIES WITH THE CORRECT RESPONSES

I'm really sorry I'm late.

Don't worry. I have copies of them here.

1 I do apologize. I've left the files at home.

No need. The signal's always bad here.

2 I'm sorry. I've forgotten your last name.

That's all right. My train was delayed too.

3 I would like to apologize for the bad line.

Never mind. I've got myself another one.

4 I'm really sorry. I think I'm very early.

No problem. It's Carson.

5 I'm so sorry. I took your cup accidentally.

That's OK. We can have coffee first.

32.3 LISTEN TO THE AUDIO AND MARK WHETHER KARL ACCEPTS THE APOLOGIES

Yes ☐   No ✓

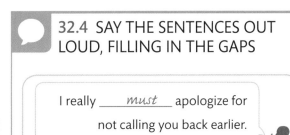
1 Yes ✓   No ☐

2 Yes ☐   No ✓

3 Yes ✓   No ☐

4 Yes ☐   No ✗

5 Yes ✓   No ☐

32.4 SAY THE SENTENCES OUT LOUD, FILLING IN THE GAPS

I really ____*must*____ apologize for not calling you back earlier.

1 I'm so _____ I was late for this morning's meeting.

2 I'm afraid that's not good _____ . I want my money back.

3 I would like to _____ for the rudeness of our receptionist.

4 That's OK, but please make _____ it doesn't happen again.

32.5 KEY LANGUAGE PAST CONTINUOUS AND PAST SIMPLE

Many workplace mistakes are caused by an unexpected
event that interrupts something else. English uses the past
continuous and past simple together to describe this.

Past continuous   Past simple

I'm so sorry. I was writing **an email when** I spilled **water on my keyboard.**

32.6 FURTHER EXAMPLES PAST CONTINUOUS AND PAST SIMPLE

I was working **on my presentation when** the CEO called **me.**

The courier was driving **to your office when** her van got **a flat tire.**

32.7 HOW TO FORM PAST CONTINUOUS AND PAST SIMPLE

The past continuous describes a longer background action, and
the past simple describes an action or event that interrupts it.

PAST CONTINUOUS	OBJECT	"WHEN"	PAST SIMPLE	REST OF SENTENCE
I was writing	an email	when	I spilled	water on my keyboar...

Use "when" to link the past
continuous and past simple.

32.8 CROSS OUT THE INCORRECT WORDS IN EACH SENTENCE

We ~~signed~~ / were signing the contract when our client ~~was receiving~~ / received a text message.

1. She was walking / walked into the room and saw that Clive practiced / was practicing his presentation.

2. I tried / was trying to make an important point when someone's phone started / was starting to ring.

3. The printer worked / was working fine when unfortunately the power went / was going off.

4. He opened / was opening the door and saw that we listened / were listening to his conversation.

5. We ate / were eating lunch in the cafeteria when we heard / were hearing the fire alarm.

32.9 READ THE EMAIL AND ANSWER THE QUESTIONS

Tam accepts that she deleted the document.
True ✓ **False** ☐ **Not given** ☐

1. Tam was working on a presentation.
True ☐ **False** ☐ **Not given** ☐

2. Tam's computer crashed yesterday.
True ☐ **False** ☐ **Not given** ☐

3. Tam was only editing a copy of the report.
True ☐ **False** ☐ **Not given** ☐

4. The company lost a client because of her mistake.
True ☐ **False** ☐ **Not given** ☐

5. Tam now regularly saves her documents.
True ☐ **False** ☐ **Not given** ☐

✉

To: Kim May

Subject: Apologies

Dear Kim,
I'm writing to apologize about the season's sales report going missing. It was entirely my fault and I really am sorry for all the disruption it caused to you and our colleagues yesterday.
I was editing the report yesterday when my computer crashed. I thought I was working on a copy of the report, so when my computer restarted, I chose not to save it. Clearly, I was working on the only master copy and accidentally deleted it from all the computers.
I will rewrite the report and now back up all my work to an external hard drive every thirty minutes so that this will not happen again.
Once again, please accept my apologies.
Best wishes,
Tam

---

33 Tasks and targets

When you are dealing with deadlines and pressure at work, you can use the present perfect to let your co-workers know how your work is progressing.

⚙ **New language** Present perfect and past simple
Aa Vocabulary Workplace tasks
🧩 **New skill** Discussing achievements at work

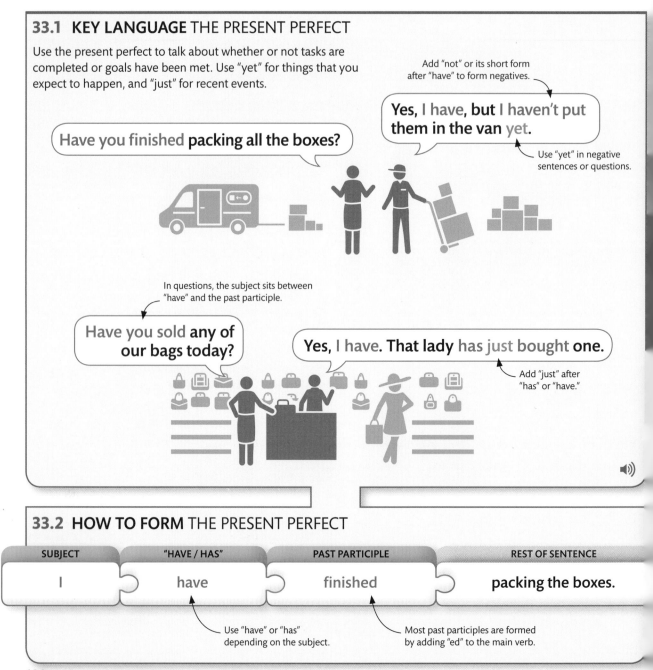

33.1 KEY LANGUAGE THE PRESENT PERFECT

Use the present perfect to talk about whether or not tasks are completed or goals have been met. Use "yet" for things that you expect to happen, and "just" for recent events.

Have you finished **packing all the boxes?**

Add "not" or its short form after "have" to form negatives.

Yes, I have, **but I haven't put them in the van** yet.

Use "yet" in negative sentences or questions.

In questions, the subject sits between "have" and the past participle.

Have you sold **any of our bags today?**

Yes, I have. **That lady** has just bought **one.**

Add "just" after "has" or "have."

33.2 HOW TO FORM THE PRESENT PERFECT

SUBJECT	"HAVE / HAS"	PAST PARTICIPLE	REST OF SENTENCE
I	have	finished	packing the boxes.

Use "have" or "has" depending on the subject.

Most past participles are formed by adding "ed" to the main verb.

33.3 FILL IN THE GAPS BY PUTTING THE VERBS IN THE PRESENT PERFECT

We _____have stopped_____ (stop) cleaning the windows because it's raining.

① Adrian _____ (make) three flower arrangements already today.

② I _____ (start) work on the report, but I won't finish it tonight.

③ Leah _____ (cut) four people's hair so far this afternoon.

④ It's early. We _____ (not speak) to any customers yet.

33.4 CROSS OUT THE INCORRECT WORD IN EACH SENTENCE

Have you finished the reports just / yet?

① I've just / yet left work and it's very late.

② We haven't shown this to the public just / yet.

③ Have you just / yet started selling this product?

④ She hasn't done her training course just / yet.

⑤ They've just / yet opened the store doors.

33.5 READ JUAN'S TO DO LIST AND ANSWER THE QUESTIONS

o do list

- Update timesheets
- File client documents
- Move files across to new server
- Call the engineer
- Book appointment with designer
- Buy coffee and tea
- Update the computer software
- Write training manual
- Renew parking permit
- Call Sam about lunch

Juan has updated his timesheets.
True ☐ **False** ☑

① Juan has called the engineer.
True ☐ **False** ☐

② Juan has bought tea and coffee.
True ☐ **False** ☐

③ Juan hasn't written the training manual.
True ☐ **False** ☐

④ Juan hasn't called Sam about lunch yet.
True ☐ **False** ☐

33.6 KEY LANGUAGE PRESENT PERFECT AND PAST SIMPLE

Use the present perfect to talk about tasks you completed recently that still have an impact in the present.

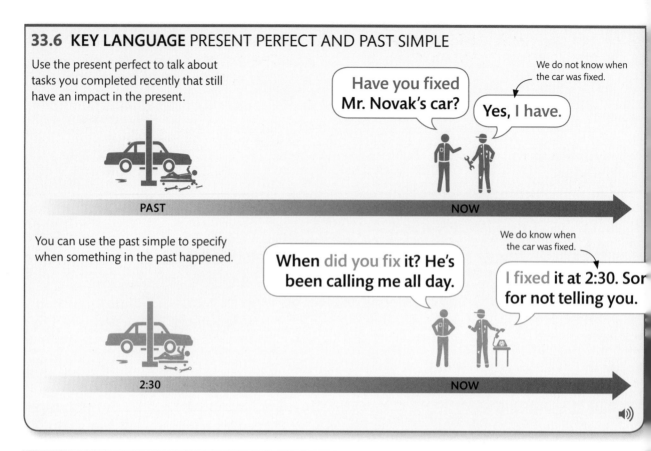

We do not know when the car was fixed.

Have you fixed Mr. Novak's car?

Yes, I have.

PAST — NOW

You can use the past simple to specify when something in the past happened.

We do know when the car was fixed.

When did you fix it? He's been calling me all day.

I fixed it at 2:30. Sor for not telling you.

2:30 — NOW

33.7 REWRITE THE SENTENCES, CORRECTING THE ERRORS

> The courier **has left** the office this morning, and your delivery will arrive today.
> *The courier left the office this morning, and your delivery will arrive today.*

❶ We've **received** your order two hours ago and sent it about an hour ago.

_____

❷ I made all those pastries this morning and **I sold** them all now.

_____

❸ **I've started** painting Ms. Malone's living room at 7 today, but I haven't finished yet.

_____

❹ I emailed the clients yesterday but they **not** replied yet.

_____

33.8 LISTEN TO THE AUDIO AND ANSWER THE QUESTIONS

Tanya and Imran are talking about their busy week at work.

What has Imran done recently?
- Left his job ☐
- Started a new job ☑
- Won a promotion ☐

1 Imran has met...
- some of his new co-workers ☐
- all his new co-workers ☐
- only his manager ☐

2 What did Imran do on Tuesday?
- He had a meeting with his boss ☐
- He met some of his co-workers ☐
- He went to a conference ☐

3 What did Tanya do this week?
- She gave a conference talk ☐
- She appeared on TV ☐
- She finished her research ☐

4 Where did Imran and Tanya both go?
- A meeting for local business ☐
- A marketing conference ☐
- A talk on local businesses ☐

5 What did they think of the last speaker?
- Only Imran liked his talk ☐
- Only Tanya liked his talk ☐
- They both liked his talk ☐

33.9 RESPOND OUT LOUD TO THE AUDIO, FILLING IN THE GAPS USING THE WORDS IN THE PANEL

Have you finished the reports?

No, I haven't finished them ___yet___ .

1 When did you start working here?

I _____ in January this year.

2 Has Clare explained the task to you?

No, she _____ yet.

3 Have you packed all the boxes yet?

Yes, I've _____ finished.

4 Who has left the meeting room so messy?

Not me. I _____ been in there.

~~yet~~	just	hasn't
haven't		started

---

34 Dealing with complaints

If a customer complains about a problem, one way to
offer a solution, and to make predictions or promises,
is to use the future with "will."

⚙ **New language** The future with "will"
Aa Vocabulary Complaints and apologies
🧩 **New skill** Dealing with complaints

34.1 KEY LANGUAGE THE FUTURE WITH "WILL"

Use the future with "will" to make a promise
to resolve a customer's problem.

Use "will" to make a promise
and offer a solution.

> I called a taxi half an hour
> ago, and it hasn't arrived yet.

> I'm very sorry about that. I will
> contact the driver immediately

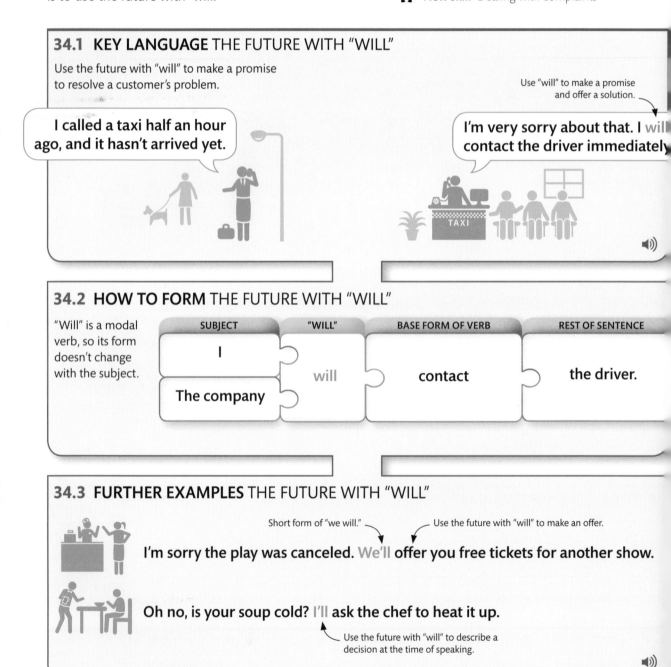

34.2 HOW TO FORM THE FUTURE WITH "WILL"

"Will" is a modal
verb, so its form
doesn't change
with the subject.

SUBJECT	"WILL"	BASE FORM OF VERB	REST OF SENTENCE
I	will	contact	the driver.
The company			

34.3 FURTHER EXAMPLES THE FUTURE WITH "WILL"

Short form of "we will." — Use the future with "will" to make an offer.

I'm sorry the play was canceled. We'll offer you free tickets for another show.

Oh no, is your soup cold? I'll ask the chef to heat it up.

Use the future with "will" to describe a
decision at the time of speaking.

34.4 READ THE LETTER AND WRITE ANSWERS TO THE QUESTIONS AS FULL SENTENCES

Dear Ms. Chang,

Thank you very much for your letter of September 24 regarding your walking tour last month. We were very upset to hear that you did not enjoy your vacation, and we take full responsibility for the problems that you experienced.

We were sorry to hear that no one responded to your phone calls on the contact number that you were given when you arrived. We will ensure that every customer is now given a second contact number. Regarding the lack of a vegetarian option in the hotel restaurant, the hotel promises that they will offer both vegetarian and vegan options from now on.

By way of an apology, we have included a voucher worth $200 off your next trip with us.

Yours sincerely,
Dylan Levine

What type of vacation did Ms. Chang go on?

She went on a walking tour.

1 How did Ms. Chang feel about her vacation?

_____

2 What was Ms. Chang's first complaint about?

_____

3 What will the company do about phone calls?

_____

4 What was Ms. Chang's second complaint?

_____

5 What will the hotel do in the future?

_____

6 What has the company given Ms. Chang?

_____

34.5 MATCH THE COMPLAINTS TO THE CORRECT RESPONSES

My train was two hours late.

1 How can I get my money back?

2 This steak is not cooked correctly.

3 These shirts are too small for me.

4 Your sales assistant was rude.

5 Where are all your wait staff?

We will refund it to your credit card.

I'll talk to him about his bad attitude.

We'll give you money off your next trip.

They'll be with you as soon as possible.

I'll take it back to the kitchen.

We'll replace them with bigger ones.

34.6 KEY LANGUAGE MAKING PREDICTIONS

You can also use "will" to make predictions about the future.

Will my taxi arrive in the next five minutes?

Yes, it will. I'm on my way now.

Use "I'm afraid" to apologize.

Short form of "will not."

No, I'm afraid it won't. The traffic is terrible.

34.7 FILL IN THE GAPS USING THE WORDS IN THE PANEL

The company will _offer_ you a discount.

1 I'm afraid your order _____ arrive today.

2 We'll _____ your appointment now.

3 I'll _____ to my manager for you.

4 We'll _____ you a replacement tomorrow.

5 I _____ contact the courier about the delay.

6 I'll _____ the chef to bring you a new meal.

7 Your delivery will _____ later today.

talk	arrive	won't
	offer	ask
will	change	send

34.8 LISTEN TO THE AUDIO AND MARK WHETHER EACH SCENARIO WILL OR WON'T HAPPEN TODAY

Will ☐ Won't ☑

1 Will ☑ Won't ☐

2 Will ☑ Won't ☐

3 Will ☑ Won't ☐

4 Will ☑ Won't ☐

5 Will ☐ Won't ☒

34.9 RESPOND OUT LOUD TO THE AUDIO, FILLING IN THE GAPS USING THE WORDS IN THE PANEL

This milk was sour when I bought it.

I'm very __sorry__ about that. Would you like a __refund__ ?

① This part is broken and it doesn't work.

I do _____ . We'll _____ the broken part for you.

② Can you send the replacement part today?

I'm _____ it _____ arrive until Wednesday.

③ My train was 90 minutes late!

We'll _____ you a _____ on your next trip.

afraid

~~refund~~

offer

apologize

won't

discount

replace

~~sorry~~

34 ⊘ CHECKLIST

✿ The future with "will" ☐   **Aa** Complaints and apologies ☐   🧩 Dealing with complaints ☐

⟳ REVIEW THE ENGLISH YOU HAVE LEARNED IN UNITS 29–34

NEW LANGUAGE	SAMPLE SENTENCE	☑	UNIT
TALKING ABOUT RULES POLITE REQUESTS	You can't wear jeans to work. Could you send your email again, please?	☐	29.1, 29.5
DESCRIBING WORKPLACE PROBLEMS	The printer wasn't working today.	☐	31.1
APOLOGIZING AND GIVING EXPLANATIONS	I'm really sorry. I was writing an email when I spilled water on my keyboard.	☐	32.1, 32.5
DISCUSSING DEADLINES	I have finished packing the boxes.	☐	33.1
DEALING WITH COMPLAINTS	We will investigate this problem, and we'll offer you a discount.	☐	34.1

35 Vocabulary

35.1 TRANSPORTATION

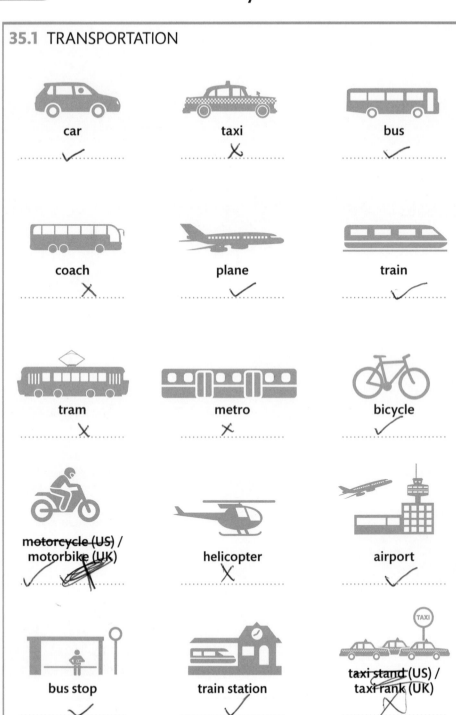

car ✓

taxi ✗

bus ✓

coach ✗

plane ✓

train ✓

tram ✗

metro ✗

bicycle ✓

motorcycle (US) / motorbike (UK) ✓

helicopter ✗

airport ✓

bus stop ✓

train station ✓

taxi stand (US) / taxi rank (UK) ✗

35.2 TRAVEL

one-way ticket

terminal

check-in

boarding pass

first class

round trip ticket (US) / return ticket (UK)

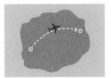 domestic flight

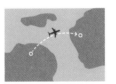 international flight

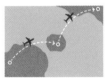 connecting flight

 on time

 late

 delay

 luggage

 security

 passport

 passport control

 departure gate

 board a plane

 seat reservation

 aisle seat

 window seat

 business class

 economy

 transfer

 hotel

36 Making travel arrangements

When you have travel plans or want to discuss the arrangements for a trip, it is useful to be able to talk about the possible results of actions and choices.

⚙ **New language** Zero and first conditional
Aa Vocabulary Travel
🧩 **New skill** Talking about actions and results

36.1 KEY LANGUAGE THE FIRST CONDITIONAL

You can use the first conditional when you want to describe a realistic action and a future result that it might lead to.

If you buy a return flight, you will save money.

🔊

36.2 HOW TO FORM THE FIRST CONDITIONAL

The first conditional is usually introduced by "if" followed by the present simple. The future with "will" expresses the result.

"IF"	PRESENT SIMPLE	COMMA	FUTURE WITH "WILL"
If	**you buy a return flight**	**,**	**you will save money.**

"If" shows that the sentence is conditional.

Present simple tense describes suggested action.

Comma separates action from result.

Future with "will" describes the result.

36.3 FURTHER EXAMPLES THE FIRST CONDITIONAL

If you book in advance, you will get a discount.

If they bring a lot of equipment, we will need a bigger suitcase.

If the trip is long, I will probably fall asleep.

We will be late for the flight **if** we don't leave soon.

You can put the "if" clause at the end of the sentence if you remove the comma.

 🔊

36.4 MATCH THE BEGINNINGS OF THE SENTENCES TO THE CORRECT ENDINGS

Will you buy a ticket ——————→ if I buy one, too?

if we land late at the airport?

you will need a taxi.

1. If you go to China for business,

2. If I go to China on business,

3. If we win the contract,

4. Will you arrange a taxi

5. We won't get a discount

6. If you have a lot of luggage,

will you visit the Great Wall?

if we don't book now.

I won't have time to go sightseeing.

we will go out to celebrate.

36.5 LISTEN TO THE AUDIO AND ANSWER THE QUESTIONS

Dan is calling his colleague, Simon, to arrange flights for a conference. They are discussing travel options.

The person making the booking is...

Dan. ☐

Dan's assistant. ☑

Simon. ☐

1. They will travel to the airport...

by train. ☐

by taxi. ☐

by bus. ☐

2. Their plane tickets will be...

Economy. ☐

Business Class. ☐

First Class. ☐

3. They will be met in Hanoi by...

a taxi driver. ☐

a former colleague. ☐

nobody. ☐

4. They will travel directly...

to the conference venue. ☐

to the hotel. ☐

to do some sightseeing. ☐

5. Dan asks Simon to send him...

the flight tickets. ☐

his passport details. ☐

his presentation. ☐

36.6 KEY LANGUAGE THE ZERO CONDITIONAL

You can use the zero conditional
to talk about things that are
generally true, or to describe the
direct result of an action.

If your bag weighs too much, **we charge a fee.**

36.7 HOW TO FORM THE ZERO CONDITIONAL

The zero conditional uses "if" or "when" with the present
simple, followed by the present simple in the main clause.

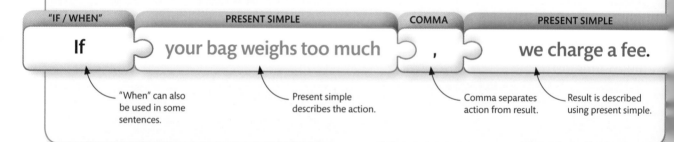

"IF / WHEN"	PRESENT SIMPLE	COMMA	PRESENT SIMPLE
If	**your bag weighs too much**	**,**	**we charge a fee.**

"When" can also
be used in some
sentences.

Present simple
describes the action.

Comma separates
action from result.

Result is described
using present simple.

36.8 FURTHER EXAMPLES THE ZERO CONDITIONAL

"When" can sometimes be
used instead of "if."

 If you book online, **flights
are often cheaper.**

 When I pack in a hurry, I
sometimes forget my passport.

 The airport has a shower if
you need to freshen up.

 Clients get angry if we
don't pay their expenses.

 The airline offers transfers if
you have a connecting flight.

 If I don't carry a map,
I always get lost in a new city.

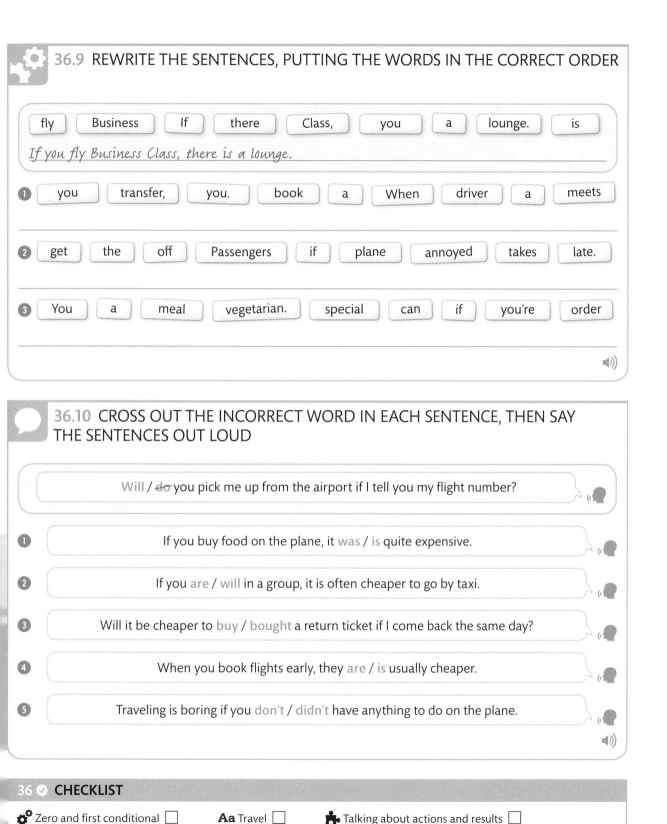

36.9 REWRITE THE SENTENCES, PUTTING THE WORDS IN THE CORRECT ORDER

| fly | Business | If | there | Class, | you | a | lounge. | is |

If you fly Business Class, there is a lounge.

1. | you | transfer, | you. | book | a | When | driver | a | meets |

---

2. | get | the | off | Passengers | if | plane | annoyed | takes | late. |

---

3. | You | a | meal | vegetarian. | special | can | if | you're | order |

36.10 CROSS OUT THE INCORRECT WORD IN EACH SENTENCE, THEN SAY THE SENTENCES OUT LOUD

Will / ~~do~~ you pick me up from the airport if I tell you my flight number?

1. If you buy food on the plane, it was / is quite expensive.

2. If you are / will in a group, it is often cheaper to go by taxi.

3. Will it be cheaper to buy / bought a return ticket if I come back the same day?

4. When you book flights early, they are / is usually cheaper.

5. Traveling is boring if you don't / didn't have anything to do on the plane.

---

36 ✓ CHECKLIST

⚙ Zero and first conditional ☐   **Aa** Travel ☐   🧩 Talking about actions and results ☐

37 Asking for directions

When traveling to conferences and meetings, you may need to ask for directions. Knowing how to be polite but clear is essential.

⚙ **New language** Imperatives, prepositions of place
Aa Vocabulary Directions
🧩 **New skill** Asking for and giving directions

37.1 KEY LANGUAGE ASKING FOR AND GIVING DIRECTIONS

When you ask for directions, be polite and listen carefully to the response. Imperatives are often used to give directions.

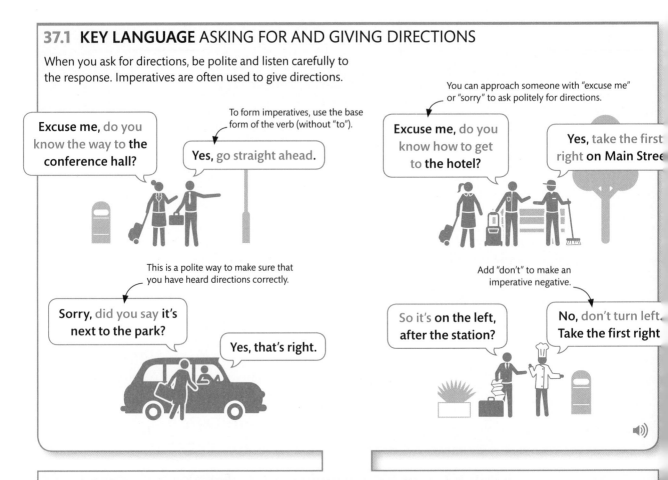

To form imperatives, use the base form of the verb (without "to").

Excuse me, do you know the way to **the conference hall?**

Yes, go straight ahead.

You can approach someone with "excuse me" or "sorry" to ask politely for directions.

Excuse me, do you know how to get to **the hotel?**

Yes, take the first right **on Main Street**

This is a polite way to make sure that you have heard directions correctly.

Sorry, did you say **it's next to the park?**

Yes, that's right.

Add "don't" to make an imperative negative.

So it's **on the left, after the station?**

No, don't turn left. Take the first right

37.2 FURTHER EXAMPLES GIVING DIRECTIONS WITH IMPERATIVES

Stop at the hotel.

Turn left at the sign.

Go past the restaurant.

Wait at the gate.

Take the second right.

37.3 VOCABULARY PREPOSITIONS OF PLACE AND OTHER DIRECTIONS

next to

opposite /
across from

between

on the corner

behind

....

in front of

on the right

on the left

intersection /
crossroads

block

....

37.4 CROSS OUT THE INCORRECT WORD IN EACH SENTENCE

It's opposite / ~~between~~ the mall downtown.

1. The venue is straight ahead and on the / a left.

2. Excuse you / me, do you know where the gym is?

3. Sorry, did you say / tell it's on the right?

4. Go straight ahead and turn / turning left.

5. The bus stop is in front of / to the park.

6. Do you know the way / where to the post office?

7. The hotel is 50 feet ahead in / on the right.

8. Do you think / know the way to the hotel?

9. Do / Go straight ahead and you'll see the sign.

10. The bus stop is directly opposite the / of bank.

11. Turn right at the intersection / block.

37.5 MARK THE SENTENCES THAT ARE CORRECT

The building is on the corner. ☑
The building is by the corner. ☐

1. Do you know how to be to Silver Street? ☐
Do you know how to get to Silver Street? ☐

2. It's in front of the red building. ☐
It's on front of the red building. ☐

3. Don't take a first right. Take the second. ☐
Don't take the first right. Take the second. ☐

4. I'll meet you across from the hotel. ☐
I'll meet you across the hotel. ☐

5. Go straight ahead and turn left at the lights. ☐
Go straight ahead and turn left on lights. ☐

6. The bank is next to the station. ☐
The bank is the next to station. ☐

37.6 REWRITE THE SENTENCES, PUTTING THE WORDS IN THE CORRECT ORDER

| way | Do | bank? | to | the | know | you | the |

Do you know the way to the bank?

① | you | Sorry, | opposite | café? | did | say | it's | the |

② | ahead | right | and | Go | turn | the | straight | at | intersection. |

③ | to | Do | know | to | you | get | the | how | venue? |

④ | past | and | post | Go | on | it's | the | left. | office | the |

◀))

37.7 LISTEN TO THE AUDIO AND MARK THE DIRECTIONS YOU HEAR

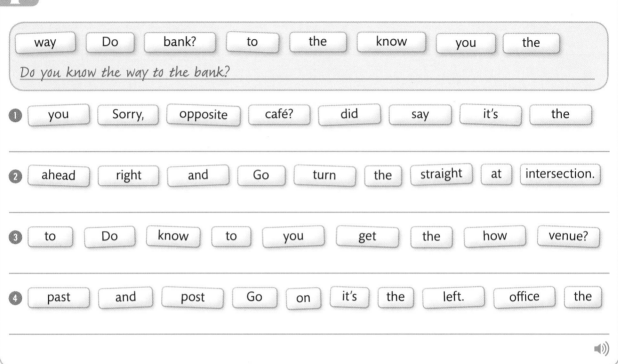

LOOK AT THE MAP, THEN RESPOND TO THE AUDIO OUT LOUD, FILLING IN THE GAPS

You are here

Do you know the way to the hospital?

Yes. Take the second ___right___ .
It's ___opposite___ the museum.

3 Can you tell me where the nearest hotel is?

Go straight _____ .
It's on the _____ .

1 Is there a restaurant near here?

Take the first _____ , and
go _____ the hotel.

4 Do you know the way to the train station?

Take the first _____ ,
then _____ straight ahead.

2 Could you tell me the way to the museum?

It's across from the hospital.
Take the _____ right.

5 Can you tell me the quickest way to a café?

Just go _____ ahead
and it's on the _____ .

38 Describing your stay

You can describe events using either active or passive sentences. The focus in a passive sentence is on the action itself rather than the thing that caused it.

⚙ **New language** The passive voice
Aa Vocabulary Hotels and accommodation
🧩 **New skill** Using the passive voice

38.1 KEY LANGUAGE THE PASSIVE VOICE

In passive sentences, the person or thing doing the action is unknown, unimportant, or obvious.

The staff served breakfast on the hotel terrace.

In this active sentence, the focus is on the people serving breakfast.

Breakfast was served on the hotel terrace.

Here the focus is on breakfast, rather than the people who served it.

🔊

38.2 HOW TO FORM THE PASSIVE VOICE

All passives use a form of "be" with a past participle. "By" can be used to introduce the person or thing doing the action.

SUBJECT	FORM OF "BE"	PAST PARTICIPLE	REST OF SENTENCE
Breakfast	**was**	**served**	**by the staff.**

The main verb is expressed as a past participle.

38.3 FURTHER EXAMPLES THE PASSIVE VOICE

 The TV was broken when I arrived.

 The hotel room was booked by my assistant.

 The Wi-Fi code is written on your keycard.

 A wake-up call was not offered.

 🔊

38.4 MATCH THE ACTIVE SENTENCES TO THE CORRECT PASSIVE VERSIONS

The guest requested a double room.	The rooms were cleaned this morning.
① Maria cleaned the rooms this morning.	The key was left in the door.
② Someone left the key in the door.	A double room was requested.
③ The CEO met the VIPs in the boardroom.	Flowers were put in the hotel foyer.
④ Someone put flowers in the hotel foyer.	The VIPs were met in the boardroom.

38.5 REWRITE THE PASSIVE SENTENCES, PUTTING THE WORDS IN THE CORRECT ORDER

opened   was   VIP.   a   hotel   by   The

The hotel was opened by a VIP.

① car   driven   chauffeur.   The   was   by   a

_____

② by   the   guest.   key   The   was   found

_____

③ shown   conference   around   They   the   venue.   were

_____

38.6 LISTEN TO THE AUDIO, THEN NUMBER THE PICTURES IN THE ORDER THEY ARE DESCRIBED

Ⓐ ☐

Ⓑ 1

Ⓒ ☐

Ⓓ ☐

38.7 READ THE REVIEWS AND ANSWER THE QUESTIONS

Hotel Gwesty is not near the airport.
True ☐ **False** ☐ **Not given** ☑

❶ Hugh Jenkins didn't like the hotel staff.
True ☐ **False** ☐ **Not given** ☐

❷ Hugh Jenkins and his clients ate at the hotel.
True ☐ **False** ☐ **Not given** ☐

❸ Hugh Jenkins will go back to Hotel Gwesty.
True ☐ **False** ☐ **Not given** ☐

❹ Sue Vardy was impressed by Hotel Plaza.
True ☐ **False** ☐ **Not given** ☐

❺ The Wi-Fi worked well at Hotel Plaza.
True ☐ **False** ☐ **Not given** ☐

❻ The furniture at Hotel Plaza was bad.
True ☐ **False** ☐ **Not given** ☐

Which hotel?

HOME | REVIEWS | ABOUT | CONTACT

Hotel Gwesty: Review by Hugh Jenkins, CEO TotalData
The hotel is very conveniently located, less than two miles from the airport. From the moment we checked in, I was impressed by the staff's professional manner. They immediately took us to the meeting room to look around before our clients arrived. The meeting room was comfortable and had all the equipment we needed for presentations and discussions. Throughout the day, we had refreshments provided in the room and an excellent buffet lunch. Our clients were happy and we will be returning here for future meetings.

Hotel Plaza: Review by Sue Vardy, Director Centria32
The best part of our stay here was checking out! We booked this hotel to launch our new product, and it was a disaster. Our conference room was very dark and there was no Wi-Fi or internet connection at all. We could not turn the projector on, the furniture was falling apart, and worst of all, they forgot to pick up our client from the airport! A horrible place!

Aa 38.8 MATCH THE DEFINITIONS TO THE CORRECT PHRASAL VERBS

arrive and register at an airport or hotel → check in

look around

❶ pick a person up in a vehicle and take them somewhere

pick up

❷ to break because something is old or poorly made

fall apart

❸ to make something work, often with a switch

check out

❹ the process of leaving a hotel after you have paid

turn on

❺ walk around a place to see what is there

38.9 LISTEN TO THE AUDIO, THEN NUMBER THE SENTENCES IN THE ORDER YOU HEAR THEM

An assistant is calling a hotel to reserve a room for her boss.

A How many rooms would you like? ☐

B Could I reserve a parking space for those days? ☐

C Would you like to book breakfast now? ☐

D I'd like to make a reservation, please. ☐ 1

E Can I have the name, please? ☐

38.10 RESPOND OUT LOUD TO THE AUDIO, PUTTING THE VERBS IN THE PASSIVE VOICE

What did you think of the meals during your stay?

The hotel food _____was prepared_____ (prepare) very badly.

1 Where did you have breakfast in the morning?

Breakfast _____ (serve) in the main restaurant.

2 Were the rooms clean and tidy?

The rooms _____ (clean) every day.

3 Who reserved your rooms?

The reservation _____ (make) by my assistant.

4 Were the rooms nice?

Yes. Very. They _____ (decorate) beautifully.

38 ✓ CHECKLIST

⚙ The passive voice ☐   **Aa** Hotels and accommodation ☐   🧩 Using the passive voice ☐

39.1 EATING OUT

chef

waiter

waitress

make a reservation / booking

menu

appetizer (US) / starter (UK)

entrée (US) / main course (UK)

dessert

check (US) / bill (UK)

receipt

café

restaurant

bar

tip

food allergy / intolerance

breakfast

lunch

dinner

vegan

vegetarian

broil (US) / grill (UK)

bake

roast

boil

fry

39.2 FOOD AND DRINK

 food ✓

 drinks ✓

 fork ✓

 knife ✓

 spoon ✓

 napkin ✓

 cup ✓

 glass ✓

 tea ✓

 coffee ✓

 water ✓

 milk ✓

 cream ✓

 butter ✓

 cheese ✓

 meat ✓

 fish ✓

 seafood ✓

 fruit ✓

 vegetables ✓

 potatoes ✓

 rice ✓

 pasta ✓

 bread ✓

 sandwich ✓

 soup ✓

 salad ✗

 cake ✓

 chocolate ✓

 sugar ✓

40 Conferences and visitors

Whether you are welcoming visitors, or visiting somewhere on business yourself, it is important to know how to interact politely in English.

⚙️ **New language** "A," "some," "any"
Aa Vocabulary Hospitality
🧩 **New skill** Welcoming visitors

40.1 KEY LANGUAGE WELCOMING VISITORS

There are a number of phrases you can use when welcoming visitors who have come to see you on business.

Welcome **to Hanoi.**

Have you been **to Hanoi before?**

You must be **Mr. Burford.**

Yes, we spoke on the phone.

It's great to meet in person.

Did you have a good flight?

Can I get you anything?

🔊

40.2 MARK THE SENTENCES THAT ARE CORRECT

You are Mr. Draper.	☐
You must be Mr. Draper.	☑

① Yes, we speak on the phone. ☐
Yes, we spoke on the phone. ☐

② Have you been to Mexico City before? ☐
Have you been Mexico City before? ☐

③ I'll let Mrs. Singh know that you're here. ☐
I'll tell Mrs. Singh know you're here. ☐

④ Would you like some tea or coffee? ☐
Would you have some tea or coffee? ☐

⑤ Did you have a good flight? ☐
Did you have a well flight? ☐

⑥ I've been looking forward to this visit. ☐
I've been look forward to this visit. ☐

⑦ It's great to meet your person. ☐
It's great to meet you in person. ☐

⑧ Did you have any trouble getting here? ☐
Do you have any trouble getting here? ☐

⑨ Can I get you anything? ☐
Can I have you anything? ☐

🔊

40.3 KEY LANGUAGE "A," "SOME," "ANY"

In English, nouns can either be countable, meaning they can be easily counted, or uncountable, meaning they aren't usually counted individually. Use "a" or "an" with single countable nouns. Use "some" with plural countable nouns and uncountable nouns. Use "any" in questions and negative statements.

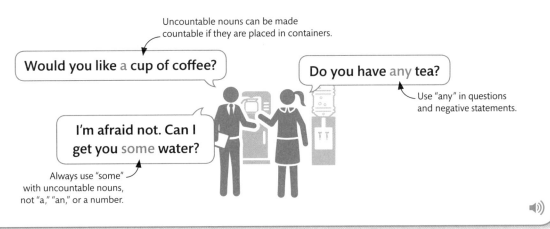

Uncountable nouns can be made countable if they are placed in containers.

Would you like a cup of coffee?

Do you have any tea?

Use "any" in questions and negative statements.

I'm afraid not. Can I get you some water?

Always use "some" with uncountable nouns, not "a," "an," or a number.

40.4 REWRITE SENTENCES, CORRECTING THE ERRORS

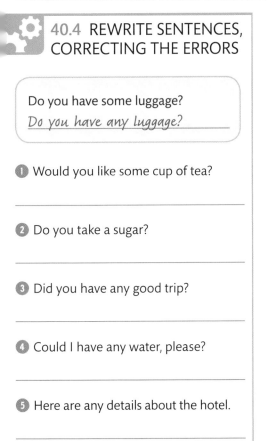

Do you have some luggage?
Do you have any luggage?

❶ Would you like some cup of tea?

_____

❷ Do you take a sugar?

_____

❸ Did you have any good trip?

_____

❹ Could I have any water, please?

_____

❺ Here are any details about the hotel.

_____

40.5 MATCH THE BEGINNINGS OF THE SENTENCES TO THE CORRECT ENDINGS

| I like to drink | a good flight? |

❶ I didn't bring — any help?

❷ Did you have — coffee at breakfast.

❸ Do you need — any luggage.

❹ Would you like to — anything to drink?

❺ There will be — meet the team?

❻ Can I get you — seat and wait here.

❼ Please take a — something to eat.

149

40.6 LISTEN TO THE AUDIO AND ANSWER THE QUESTIONS

Two attendees are discussing products at a marketing conference in Hanoi.

1 When was the conference's opening reception?
The morning before ☐
The evening before ☐
That morning ☐

2 What does Ben Park want to see at the conference?
A product launch ☐
Jo's presentation ☐
The closing session ☐

3 What is Jo going to give a presentation about?
Networking at conferences ☐
Social media and marketing ☐
A new product launch ☐

Where has Mr. Park traveled from?
London ☐
Moscow ☑
Seoul ☐

Aa 40.7 FILL IN THE GAPS USING THE WORDS IN THE PANEL

Collect your lanyard from ___reception___ .

1 The _____ speech will start at 10am.

2 The main _____ used a lot of slides.

3 The main sponsor will _____ a new product.

4 Every attendee gets a _____ and a name tag.

5 In a workshop the _____ get involved.

6 There are lots of _____ opportunities.

reception   keynote

launch   lanyard   networking

delegates   presenter

◀))

⚙ 40.8 CROSS OUT THE INCORRECT WORDS IN EACH SENTENCE

There is a / ~~any~~ / ~~some~~ workshop at midday.

1 They have a / some / any free food and drinks.

2 Do you have a / some / any lanyard already?

3 I have a / some / any business cards to give people.

4 I'd like to see a / some / any interesting talks.

5 Are you going to a / some / any talks today?

6 Do you have a / some / any business card?

7 Are you staying in a / some / any hotel?

8 They don't have a / some / any drinks.

9 I'm giving a / some / any presentation today.

◀))

40.9 READ THE ARTICLE AND MARK THE CORRECT SUMMARY

Conference tips:

1 Use conferences to network. Dress professionally, act politely, and tell everyone all about yourself. ☐

2 Use conferences to network. Dress professionally, act politely, and find out about the person you are talking to. ☐

3 Use conferences to network. Dress professionally, act politely, and tell your clients about yourself. ☐

Going to a conference is one of the best ways to network and make new business connections.

• It is really important to make a good first impression. Remember, you might be talking to a future client or employer.

• Dress professionally and always behave politely. Most importantly, show an interest in the person you are talking to. Find out their name; ask them what they do and ask about their family. This, in turn, will make them more likely to ask about you.

40.10 RESPOND OUT LOUD TO THE AUDIO, FILLING IN THE GAPS USING THE WORDS IN THE PANEL

Do you have any goals for the conference?

I want to start _____*networking*_____ with people in my field.

1 Sorry, I didn't catch your name.

It's Leo Smart. I haven't collected my _____ yet.

2 Do you have any contact details?

Yes, here. Please take my _____ .

3 Are you going to any presentations?

Yes, and I went to an interesting _____ this morning.

workshop

business card

~~networking~~

lanyard

41 Dining and hospitality

It is important to learn local customs for dining and entertaining. At business lunches and conferences, follow these customs and use polite language.

⚙ **New language** "Much / many," "too / enough"
Aa **Vocabulary** Restaurants
🧩 **New skill** Offering and accepting hospitality

41.1 KEY LANGUAGE DINING IN RESTAURANTS

When dining or sharing hospitality with clients, it is important as a host or guest to be friendly and polite.

I'd like a table for two, please.

Do you have a reservation?

Yes. My name is Sarah Key.

Do you have any tables free for lunch?

How many people are in your party?

I'm afraid there is a 20-minute wait.

"Could" is more polite than "can."

Are you ready to order?

Could I have the fish?

I'll have the soup, please.

Do you have any allergies?

Yes. I'm allergic to peanuts.

Add "please" to make requests more polite.

How is everything?

There were lots of bones in my fish.

Could we have the check, please?

I don't have enough cash. C I pay by card

There is too much cream in my soup.

This is usually referred to as the "bill" in UK English.

41.2 REWRITE THE SENTENCES, PUTTING THE WORDS IN THE CORRECT ORDER

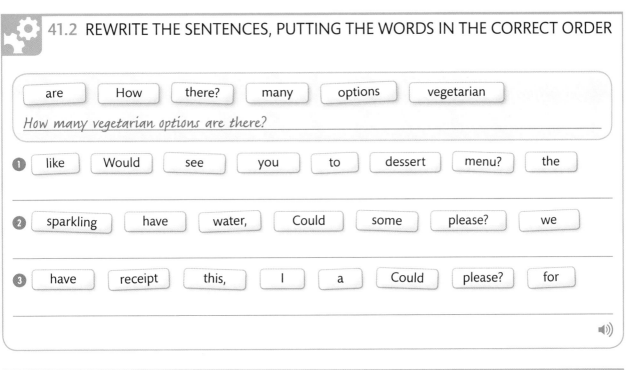

are | How | there? | many | options | vegetarian

How many vegetarian options are there?

① like | Would | see | you | to | dessert | menu? | the

_____

② sparkling | have | water, | Could | some | please? | we

_____

③ have | receipt | this, | I | a | Could | please? | for

_____

41.3 RESPOND OUT LOUD TO THE AUDIO, FILLING IN THE GAPS USING THE WORDS IN THE PANEL

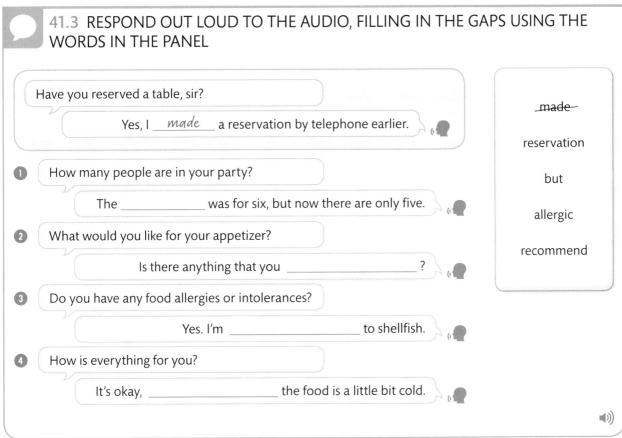

Have you reserved a table, sir?

Yes, I __made__ a reservation by telephone earlier.

① How many people are in your party?

The _____ was for six, but now there are only five.

② What would you like for your appetizer?

Is there anything that you _____ ?

③ Do you have any food allergies or intolerances?

Yes. I'm _____ to shellfish.

④ How is everything for you?

It's okay, _____ the food is a little bit cold.

made
reservation
but
allergic
recommend

41.4 KEY LANGUAGE TALKING ABOUT QUANTITY

Use "much," "many," and "enough" to talk about amounts and quantities.
These words can also show our feelings about the amounts and quantities.
For example, "too much" is negative, but "enough" is positive.

How much **time do we have?**

Use "much" to ask questions about
quantities of uncountable nouns.

How many **sides have you ordered?**

Use "many" to ask questions about
quantities of countable nouns.

There is too much **chili in this!**

"Too much / many" is used to talk about
quantities that are too large.

There aren't enough **waiters.**

"Enough" and "not enough" are used to talk
about countable and uncountable nouns.

41.5 MARK THE SENTENCES THAT ARE CORRECT

How many glasses will you need? ☑
How much glasses will you need? ☐

1. How much rice do you want? ☐
   How many rice do you want? ☐

2. I don't need more. There's enough here. ☐
   I don't need more. There's not enough here. ☐

3. There are too much seats here. ☐
   There are too many seats here. ☐

4. There's not enough water. ☐
   There's not many water. ☐

5. $40 for a steak! That's too many. ☐
   $40 for a steak! That's too much. ☐

41.6 FILL IN THE GAPS USING THE WORDS IN THE PANEL

Do you have ____enough____ bread?

1. I've eaten _____ many chocolates.

2. How _____ glasses do we need?

3. There's too _____ sauce on this.

4. How _____ should we tip here?

much	much	many
	too	~~enough~~

41.7 READ THE ARTICLE AND ANSWER THE QUESTIONS

You should ask all clients to business lunches.
True ☐ **False** ☐ **Not given** ☑

① The author recommends reading about local customs.
True ☐ **False** ☐ **Not given** ☐

② Guests should be given a selection of places to eat.
True ☐ **False** ☐ **Not given** ☐

③ You should go outside to answer your phone.
True ☐ **False** ☐ **Not given** ☐

④ Guests shouldn't order the most expensive meal.
True ☐ **False** ☐ **Not given** ☐

⑤ The author suggests you shouldn't eat too much.
True ☐ **False** ☐ **Not given** ☐

MEALS AND DEALS

Business lunches can be a great way to get to know your clients, but be careful about who you invite to lunch. CEOs, for example, have busy schedules, and it may be better to invite them for coffee. If you do invite someone to lunch, you should read about the local dining etiquette. You could also present your guest with several dining options before making a restaurant reservation. Once you arrive at the restaurant, turn off your phone. Your guests should have all your attention. If you are a guest yourself, arrive on time, and make sure that you do not order the most expensive thing on the menu. Last, as host or guest, try to enjoy yourself.

---

41 ✓ CHECKLIST

⚙ "Much / many," "too / enough" ☐   **Aa** Restaurants ☐   🧩 Offering and accepting hospitality ☐

♲ REVIEW THE ENGLISH YOU HAVE LEARNED IN UNITS 35–41

NEW LANGUAGE	SAMPLE SENTENCE	☑	UNIT
THE FIRST CONDITIONAL	If you buy a return flight, you will save money.	☐	36.1
THE ZERO CONDITIONAL	If your bag weighs too much, we charge a fee.	☐	36.6
GIVING DIRECTIONS WITH IMPERATIVES	Go straight ahead.	☐	37.1
THE PASSIVE VOICE	Breakfast was served on the hotel terrace.	☐	38.1
"A," "SOME," "ANY"	Do you have any tea? Would you like a cup of coffee or some water?	☐	40.3
"MUCH / MANY," "TOO / ENOUGH"	How much time do we have? There are not enough waiters.	☐	41.4

Informal phone calls

In most workplaces, you can use polite but informal language to call your co-workers. English often uses two- or three-part verbs in informal telephone language.

⚙ **New language** Telephone language
Aa Vocabulary Phone numbers and etiquette
🧩 **New skill** Calling your co-workers

42.1 KEY LANGUAGE MAKING INFORMAL PHONE CALLS

Informal phone calls between co-workers often use various polite phrases for starting and ending a call and exchanging information.

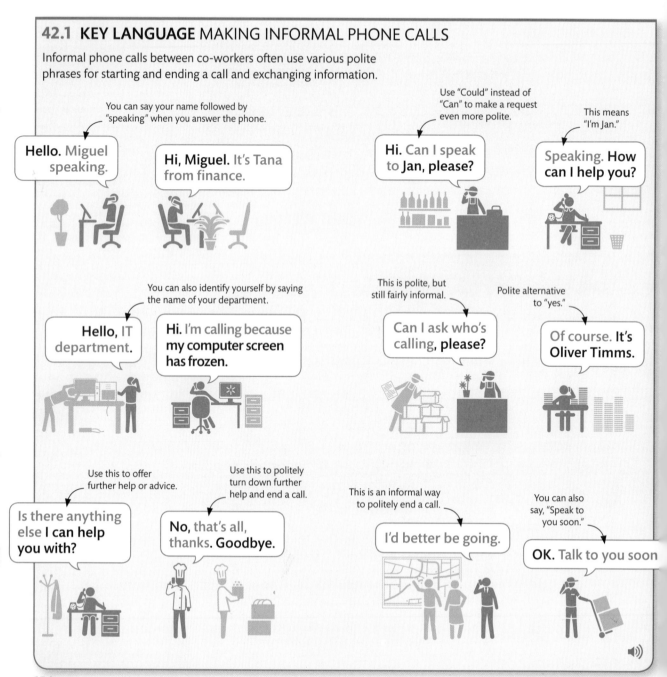

You can say your name followed by "speaking" when you answer the phone.

Hello. Miguel speaking.

Hi, Miguel. It's Tana from finance.

Use "Could" instead of "Can" to make a request even more polite.

Hi. Can I speak to Jan, please?

This means "I'm Jan."

Speaking. How can I help you?

You can also identify yourself by saying the name of your department.

Hello, IT department.

Hi. I'm calling because **my computer screen has frozen.**

This is polite, but still fairly informal.

Can I ask who's calling, **please?**

Polite alternative to "yes."

Of course. It's Oliver Timms.

Use this to offer further help or advice.

Is there anything else I can help you with?

Use this to politely turn down further help and end a call.

No, that's all, **thanks. Goodbye.**

This is an informal way to politely end a call.

I'd better be going.

You can also say, "Speak to you soon."

OK. Talk to you soon

42.2 FILL IN THE GAPS USING THE WORDS IN THE PANEL

Can I ____speak____ to Jan, please?

1 Hi, Karl. It's Katie _____ HR.

2 Hi. I'm _____ about the Wi-Fi.

3 My client is here. I'd _____ be going.

4 Can I ask _____ calling, please?

5 Is there _____ else I can do for you?

6 Hello. Olga _____ .

7 No, thanks. That's _____ . Bye.

---

better   ~~from~~   who's

anything   all

~~speak~~   calling   speaking

🔊

42.3 LISTEN TO THE AUDIO, THEN NUMBER THE SENTENCES IN THE ORDER YOU HEAR THEM

 Danny calls the IT department to discuss a problem with his computer.

Ⓐ Hi, Danny. How can I help? ☐

Ⓑ Thanks again. Talk to you soon. ☐

Ⓒ I know it's down. I've just reset the router. ☐

Ⓓ Hi, Sandra. It's Danny from sales. ☐ 1

Ⓔ Is there anything else I can help you with? ☐

Ⓕ I'm calling about the internet. ☐

42.4 SAY THE SENTENCES OUT LOUD, CORRECTING THE ERRORS

I'd better be go. Goodbye.

> *I'd better be going. Goodbye.* 🔊

1 Hi. Can I speak Jacob, please?

[   ] 🔊

2 Hello, Sophie. Here Ahmed from sales.

[   ] 🔊

3 Could I say who's calling, please?

[   ] 🔊

4 Hi. Adam speaks.

[   ] 🔊

5 It's Sandy off IT.

[   ] 🔊

6 Hi. I call because the elevator is stuck.

[   ] 🔊

7 Bye then. Speaking to you soon.

[   ] 🔊

8 Can I ask who calls, please?

[   ] 🔊

🔊

42.5 KEY LANGUAGE SAYING YOUR PHONE NUMBER

There are many useful phrases for telling people your phone number.

Informal English usually shortens "phone number" to "number."

The office number is **0078 555 251.**

An extension is the last few digits of an employee's office phone number.

My extension is **3827.**

You can also say "You can call me."

You can contact m at **603-902-0691.**

42.6 PRONUNCIATION NUMBERS

In US English, the number 0 is pronounced "zero," and repeated numbers are said individually.
In UK English, many different pronunciations are possible for 0 and rows of repeated numbers.

zero | "oh"

0

nought

four four | forty-four

44

double four

five five five | treble five

555

triple five | five double five

42.7 LISTEN TO THE AUDIO AND WRITE DOWN THE TELEPHONE NUMBERS THAT YOU HEAR

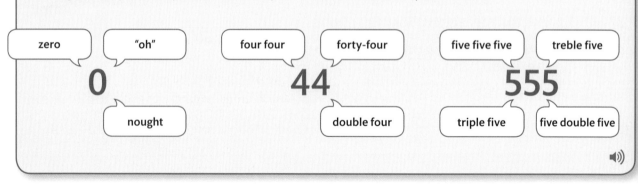

0 7 8 8 4 0 9 6 6 2

❶ _____

❷ _____

❸ _____

❹ _____

❺ _____

❻ _____

❼ _____

42.8 CROSS OUT THE INCORRECT WORD IN EACH SENTENCE, THEN SAY THE SENTENCES OUT LOUD

If you want to arrange a meeting, you **can** / ~~will~~ contact me on 0078 555 251.

1. **Can** / **Don't** you call Martin at the office? His number's 902-555-4349.

2. You **can** / **will** call me on my cell phone any time. My number's 03069 991332.

3. Hi, it's Myra. **Can** / **Do** you call me back? My number's 07064 881206.

4. **Would** / **Can** you be able to call me back? I'm at the office. My extension is 8762.

5. If you **want** / **should** to contact Samuel later, his number's 01632 960441.

6. I've got a number for Hanna if you **can** / **want** to contact her. It's 321-554-8933.

42.9 LISTEN TO THE AUDIO AND ANSWER THE QUESTIONS

Tara calls her co-worker, Sven, to ask for help with some workplace problems.

What department does Sven work in?
Sales ☐
IT ☑
HR ☐

1. What is Tara working on at the moment?
A project selling mobile devices ☐
A project selling shoes ☐
A project selling apps ☐

2. What is her main problem?
The mobile devices do not work ☐
The Wi-Fi does not work ☐
She cannot connect to the Wi-Fi ☐

3. What is Sven's solution?
Enter a different passcode ☐
Turn them off and on again ☐
Come to a different office ☐

4. What is the passcode that Sven gives?
JG330XS ☐
GJ330XF ☐
GJ330XS ☐

5. What does Sven say about Tara's second problem?
He cannot fix it ☐
She cannot fix it ☐
He will fix it ☐

42.10 KEY LANGUAGE VERBS FOR PHONE CALLS

Informal spoken English, particularly in telephone language, often uses two- or three-part verbs.

> I have to hang up now, but I'll call you back tomorrow.

42.11 FURTHER EXAMPLES VERBS FOR PHONE CALLS

I'll just put you through to the IT department.

This line is awful! I just got cut off.

Sorry, I'm really busy. Can I get back to you in 10 minutes?

Their receptionist never picks up the phone.

42.12 CROSS OUT THE INCORRECT WORDS IN EACH SENTENCE

This line is terrible! I hope we don't get cut ~~up~~ / off / ~~on~~.

1 Anna, can I call you off / on / back later from the office?

2 Suzanna always takes ages to pick up / on / off the phone.

3 Ethan, I will get back to / with / until you later with an answer.

4 I'll put you in / back / through to Ivor now.

5 If a customer is very rude, you can hang on / off / up.

6 I'll find out the information and get off / back / on to you.

7 I'm busy now, Valeria, but I'll call you / me / us back later.

| to | get | later | back | Can | you | today? | I |

Can I get back to you later today?

① | I'll | through | sales. | you | put | to | Simone | in |

_____

② | will | you | afternoon. | back | I | call | this | later |

_____

③ | just | were | off. | cut | about | we | Sorry | that; |

_____

🔊

Aa 42.14 READ THE ARTICLE AND WRITE THE HIGHLIGHTED PHRASES NEXT TO THEIR DEFINITIONS

| end a call | = | _hang up_ |

① have a call interrupted = _____

② answer the phone = _____

③ talk louder = _____

④ return your call = _____

⑤ becoming bad quality = _____

⑥ call them again = _____

Problem phone call?

What to do with people who won't stop talking

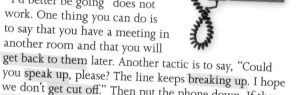

We have all wanted to **hang up** on callers who keep talking when we are really busy at work. Sometimes, the usual, "I'd better be going" does not work. One thing you can do is to say that you have a meeting in another room and that you will **get back to them** later. Another tactic is to say, "Could you **speak up**, please? The line keeps **breaking up**. I hope we don't **get cut off**." Then put the phone down. If they **call you back**, don't **pick up** the phone!

🔊

---

42 ✔ **CHECKLIST**

⚙ Telephone language ☐   **Aa** Phone numbers and etiquette ☐   👥 Calling your co-workers ☐

43 Formal phone calls

When you talk to clients or receptionists, you may
need to use formal language on the phone. You
may also need to take or leave a phone message.

⚙ **New language** Adjective order
Aa Vocabulary Formal telephone language
🧩 **New skill** Leaving phone messages

43.1 KEY LANGUAGE FORMAL PHONE CONVERSATIONS

You can use formal language to introduce yourself,
greet the speaker, and take or leave a message.

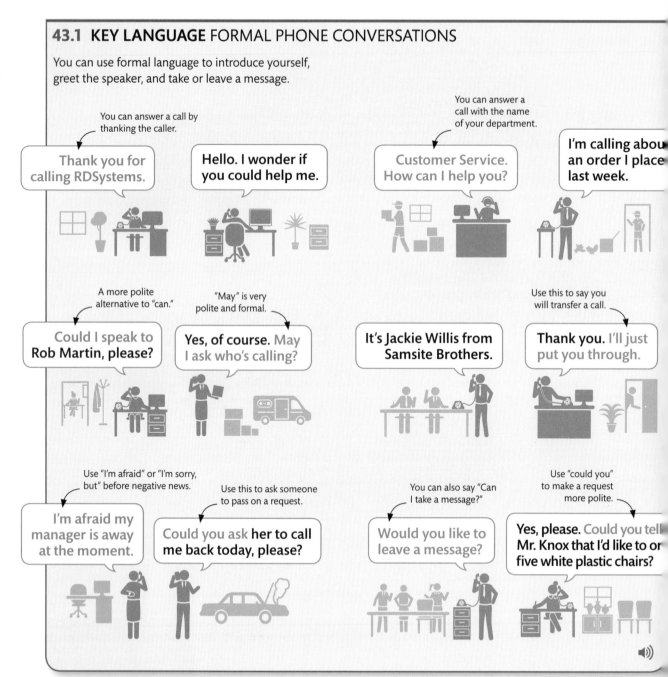

You can answer a call by
thanking the caller.

**Thank you for
calling RDSystems.**

**Hello. I wonder if
you could help me.**

You can answer a
call with the name
of your department.

**Customer Service.
How can I help you?**

**I'm calling abou
an order I place
last week.**

A more polite
alternative to "can."

**Could I speak to
Rob Martin, please?**

"May" is very
polite and formal.

**Yes, of course. May
I ask who's calling?**

**It's Jackie Willis from
Samsite Brothers.**

Use this to say you
will transfer a call.

**Thank you. I'll just
put you through.**

Use "I'm afraid" or "I'm sorry,
but" before negative news.

**I'm afraid my
manager is away
at the moment.**

Use this to ask someone
to pass on a request.

**Could you ask her to call
me back today, please?**

You can also say "Can
I take a message?"

**Would you like to
leave a message?**

Use "could you"
to make a request
more polite.

**Yes, please. Could you tell
Mr. Knox that I'd like to or
five white plastic chairs?**

43.2 MARK THE BEST REPLY TO EACH STATEMENT

Could I speak to Jia Li, please?

May I ask who's calling, please? ✓

Who are you? ☐

1 Would you like to leave a message?

I'll just put you through to HR. ☐

Can you say that I'll arrive late? ☐

2 Thank you for calling TCE Consulting.

I want the sales department. ☐

Could I speak to someone in sales? ☐

3 I'm afraid my manager is out of the office.

Can I talk to the manager? ☐

Can I leave a message for her? ☐

4 Could I talk to Myra Singh, please?

I'll get her now. ☐

Certainly. I'll just put you through. ☐

5 Customer service department. How can I help you?

Yes, please. ☐

I have a problem with an order. ☐

6 Thank you for calling EcoTech.

I'll just put you through. ☐

Hello. I wonder if you could help me. ☐

🔊))

43.3 CROSS OUT THE INCORRECT WORD IN EACH SENTENCE, THEN SAY THE SENTENCES OUT LOUD

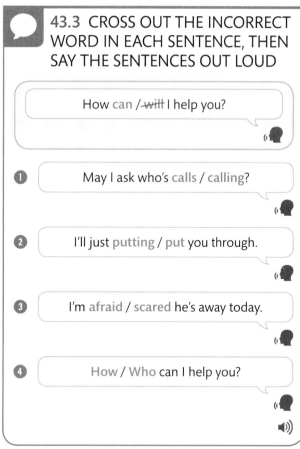

How can / ~~will~~ I help you?

1 May I ask who's calls / calling?

2 I'll just putting / put you through.

3 I'm afraid / scared he's away today.

4 How / Who can I help you?

🔊))

43.4 LISTEN TO THE AUDIO AND MARK THE CORRECT SUMMARY

Tom calls his client, Mr. Ryder, to arrange a meeting.

1 Tom and Mr. Ryder agree to meet at noon on Wednesday next week. ☐

2 Mr. Ryder is not at his desk. Tom leaves a message with the receptionist saying he will call again tomorrow. ☐

3 Mr. Ryder is not at his desk. Tom leaves a message with the receptionist saying he will meet him next week. ☐

43.5 KEY LANGUAGE ADJECTIVE ORDER

Adjectives add detail to descriptions and messages. When English uses more than one adjective before a noun, the adjectives must go in a particular order.

I've booked our team lunch at the **nice little** restaurant next to the office.

Adjectives describing opinions come before adjectives describing facts.

There's a **large red** car in the CEO's parking space. The driver needs to move it.

Fact adjectives also have their own order, depending on the type of fact.

43.6 KEY LANGUAGE ADJECTIVE ORDER IN DETAIL

English very rarely uses more than three adjectives before a noun.

	OPINION	SIZE	AGE	COLOR	MATERIAL	NOUN
I've booked the	nice	little				restaurant
These are				white	plastic	chairs.
There's a		large		red		car.
We sell	beautiful		antique		china	cups.

43.7 WRITE THE WORDS FROM THE PANEL IN THE CORRECT GROUPS

OPINION	SIZE	AGE	COLOR	MATERIAL
useful		*Ten*		

awful   large   ~~useful~~   tiny   antique

blue   wooden   new   glass   green

43.8 REWRITE THE SENTENCES, CORRECTING THE ERRORS

I have a tiny awful old desk in my office.
I have an awful tiny old desk in my office.

① My boss has a white large friendly cat.
_____

② My computer is a old white huge desktop from 1995.
_____

③ We're marketing a clever watch tiny new that helps you get fit.
_____

④ Have you seen the black tiny amazing briefcase she has?
_____

⑤ The meeting room has a modern painting very large.
_____

🔊

43.9 LISTEN TO THE AUDIO AND ANSWER THE QUESTIONS

Julio takes a phone message from Mrs. Garcia, who wants to complain about an order that she has placed.

Julio's manager isn't at her desk.
True ☑ **False** ☐ **Not given** ☐

① Mrs. Garcia ordered an old coffee pot.
True ☐ **False** ☐ **Not given** ☐

② Mrs. Garcia's items are broken.
True ☐ **False** ☐ **Not given** ☐

③ Mrs. Garcia does not like the color purple.
True ☐ **False** ☐ **Not given** ☐

④ Julio will send a replacement coffee pot.
True ☐ **False** ☐ **Not given** ☐

⑤ Mrs. Garcia must go to the post office.
True ☐ **False** ☐ **Not given** ☐

⑥ Julio will tell his manager about the call.
True ☐ **False** ☐ **Not given** ☐

43 ⊘ CHECKLIST

⚙ Adjective order ☐   **Aa** Formal telephone language ☐   🧩 Leaving phone messages ☐

44 Writing a résumé

A résumé (or CV in UK English) is a clear summary of your skills and career history. Past simple action verbs are particularly useful for describing past achievements.

⚙ **New language** Action verbs for achievements
Aa Vocabulary Résumé vocabulary
🧩 **New skill** Writing a résumé

44.1 KEY LANGUAGE RÉSUMÉ HEADINGS

Shown below are the most common English résumé headings, and useful phrases for describing your achievements.

TIP
English résumés often leave the subject and the verb "be" out of sentence. For example, "Fluent in English, Spanish, and Italian" omits "I am."

Adriana Pires

275 Main Street, Minneapolis, MN 55401
addi123@pires456.com · 612-555-1746

An introductory statement describing a person's skills, qualities, and career goals.

PERSONAL STATEMENT
A highly motivated individual, with a proven track record in hotel reception and front-of-house work.

Describes the most significant things achieved throughout someone's career.

PROFESSIONAL ACHIEVEMENTS
Won an award for the Best Hotel Receptionist in the Midwestern Region.

A list of current and previous jobs, responsibilities, and skills.

CAREER SUMMARY
Hotel Deluxe Cite
HEAD RECEPTIONIST · May 2013–Present
• Working in a service-oriented environment
• Gained in-depth knowledge of the hospitality industry, and hands-on experience in customer service.

A list of qualifications, and the institutions where they were gained.

EDUCATION
• BA in Tourism and Hospitality
• Minor in Spanish

Other important skills, such as language skills or IT skills.

KEY SKILLS
• Fluent in Portuguese, Spanish, and English
• Proficient in IT use, including most types of booking systems

Things that someone enjoys doing in his or her spare time.

INTERESTS
Cooking, traveling, paragliding, scuba diving

A reference is a recommendation from a current or previous employer.

References available upon request

166

Aa 44.2 MATCH THE PHRASES TO THE CORRECT RÉSUMÉ HEADINGS

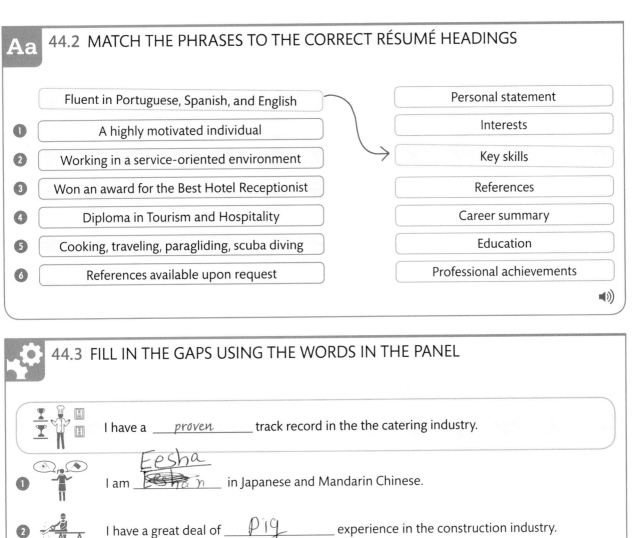

Fluent in Portuguese, Spanish, and English

1 A highly motivated individual

2 Working in a service-oriented environment

3 Won an award for the Best Hotel Receptionist

4 Diploma in Tourism and Hospitality

5 Cooking, traveling, paragliding, scuba diving

6 References available upon request

Personal statement

Interests

Key skills

References

Career summary

Education

Professional achievements

44.3 FILL IN THE GAPS USING THE WORDS IN THE PANEL

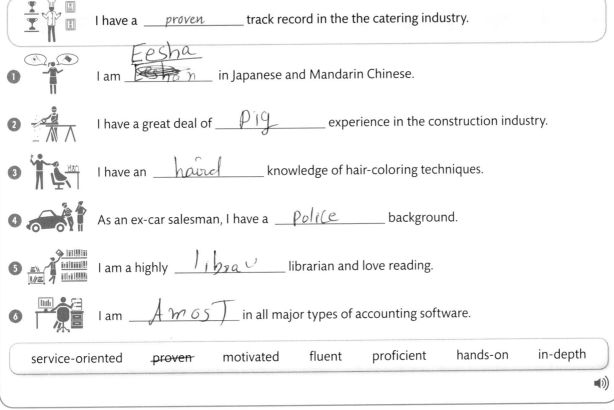

I have a ___proven___ track record in the the catering industry.

1 I am ___Eesha___ in Japanese and Mandarin Chinese.

2 I have a great deal of ___Pig___ experience in the construction industry.

3 I have an ___haird___ knowledge of hair-coloring techniques.

4 As an ex-car salesman, I have a ___Police___ background.

5 I am a highly ___librav___ librarian and love reading.

6 I am ___Amost___ in all major types of accounting software.

service-oriented   ~~proven~~   motivated   fluent   proficient   hands-on   in-depth

44.4 KEY LANGUAGE PAST SIMPLE ACTION VERBS

Use past simple action verbs on your résumé to talk about the
responsibilities you have had and your past achievements.

I managed a successful
team of scientists.

I coordinated
a major product launch.

I negotiated a great price for
the company's products.

I volunteered
in a local school.

I established a
new training program.

I collaborated with designers
to produce the company logo.

🔊

44.5 CROSS OUT THE INCORRECT WORD IN EACH SENTENCE

Last year, I managed / ~~negotiated~~ a small team of painters.

❶ Our teams established / collaborated to create the packaging design.

❷ We established / collaborated a new headquarters downtown.

❸ I coordinated / collaborated a staff training day for all departments.

❹ I managed / volunteered for a charity and built a classroom.

❺ I established / negotiated with all our suppliers and cut costs by 15 percent.

🔊

44.6 READ THE RÉSUMÉ AND ANSWER THE QUESTIONS

Ela Babinski

7 Gold Street
Perth
1609
elabab765@babela12.com
+61 491 570 156

I am determined and enthusiastic with practical experience in arranging and running sporting and educational activities for young adults. I have organized and supervised a number of overseas activity vacations in various countries and I have numerous health and safety certificates.

Career summary

YLHS Activity Vacations
HEAD OF ACTIVITIES · April 2013–present
YLHS Activity Vacations is a small, successful company, which combines adventure vacations with language education.

Duties:
- I create and supervise safe and exciting activity programs for 14–18 year-olds in three different countries.
- I manage teams of up to 16 activity leaders.

World Youth Language Schools
ACTIVITY LEADER · November 2011–April 2013
World Youth Language Schools run language courses around the world. Each day students have lessons followed by a sports activity.

Duties:
- I supervised up to 15 students at a time for activities.
- I also arranged transportation for students to and from each activity.

Professional achievements
Voted "Activity Leader of the Year" three years in a row by co-workers

Education
- Certificate in Activity Leadership, Level 3
- International Baccalaureate Diploma

Key skills
- Fluent in French and intermediate level Spanish
- First aid qualified
- Excellent organizer and people manager

Interests
Canoeing, climbing, and photography.

All the activities Ela organizes are in France.
True ☐ False ☐ Not given ✓

① Ela currently manages other activity leaders.
True ☐ False ☐ Not given ☐

② Ela's co-workers voted for her to receive an award.
True ☐ False ☐ Not given ☐

③ Ela was a language teacher for World Youth.
True ☐ False ☐ Not given ☐

④ Ela got her Activity Leadership Certificate last year.
True ☐ False ☐ Not given ☐

⑤ Ela can speak French and Spanish fluently.
True ☐ False ☐ Not given ☐

---

44 ✓ CHECKLIST

⚙ Action verbs for achievements ☐   **Aa** Résumé vocabulary ☐   ✦ Writing a résumé ☐

45 Making plans

English uses the future with "going to" to talk about plans and decisions that have already been made. It is useful for informing co-workers about your plans.

⚙ **New language** The future with "going to"
Aa Vocabulary Polite requests
🧩 **New skill** Making arrangements and plans

45.1 KEY LANGUAGE THE FUTURE WITH "GOING TO"

Use "going to" to tell co-workers what you have decided to do in the future.

I am going to arrange a training course.

45.2 HOW TO FORM THE FUTURE WITH "GOING TO"

To form the future with "going to" use the verb "to be" with "going to" followed by the base verb.

SUBJECT	"TO BE"	"GOING TO"	BASE FORM OF VERB	REST OF SENTENCE
I	am			
You / We / They	are	going to	arrange	a training course.
He / She	is			

"Going to" doesn't change with the subject.

45.3 FURTHER EXAMPLES THE FUTURE WITH "GOING TO"

They're really busy. They're not going to join us for the meeting.

Add "not" after "to be" to make the negative.

There's no paper for the printer. Are you going to order some more?

Switch the subject and "to be" in questions.

45.4 FILL IN THE GAPS USING THE FUTURE WITH "GOING TO"

I _____am going to order_____ (order) new stationery supplies this afternoon.

① They _____ (not invest) a lot of money next year.

② He _____ (travel) by plane and then taxi to the meeting.

③ _____ you _____ (meet) with the suppliers next week?

④ We _____ (buy) the best quality business cards we can.

45.5 MATCH THE PAIRS OF SENTENCES

Mr. Bassir is going to arrive at 10am.	It's good to work with different people.
① We're going to travel by plane.	Can you let her know what happens?
② She's not going to make it to the meeting.	Can you please meet him at reception?
③ We're going to give everyone leaflets.	He wants to spend more time playing golf.
④ You're going to join a new team soon.	We should email the printers today.
⑤ He's going to retire at the end of the year.	Make sure you have your passports.

45.6 LISTEN TO THE AUDIO, THEN NUMBER THE PICTURES IN THE ORDER THEY ARE DESCRIBED

Ⓐ 5̶  Ⓑ 1  Ⓒ x̶  Ⓓ 3̶  Ⓔ 2̶

45.7 KEY LANGUAGE POLITE ALTERNATIVES TO COMMANDS

Remember that it is polite to phrase requests
as questions rather than commands.

"Can" is more direct than
"could," but it is still polite.

Add "please" to make a
request more polite.

Can you **serve the refreshments, please?**

[You have to serve the refreshments.]

Use "we" instead of "you" to make
the request particularly polite.

Could we **possibly move the time of the meeting?**

[Move the time of the meeting.]

45.8 MARK THE REQUESTS THAT ARE POLITE

Please could you call our suppliers?	☑
You must call our suppliers.	☐

❶ Come to my office. ☐
Could you come to my office? ☐

❷ Why don't we discuss this at the meeting? ☐
I don't have time to discuss this now. ☐

❸ Can you tell me when it's finished, please? ☐
When will it be finished? ☐

❹ Could we move these files? ☐
Why haven't you moved these files? ☐

❺ Could you send the design to the printers? ☐
You should send the printers the design. ☐

❻ Can you help me with these figures, please? ☐
I need help with these figures. ☐

45.9 REWRITE THE SENTENCES, CORRECTING THE ERRORS

Could you to serve the refreshments?
Could you serve the refreshments?

❶ Can help you me move this cupboard?
_____

❷ Could you being a little neater, please?
_____

❸ Can you to finish the design soon, please?
_____

❹ Could us meet at 5 instead of 6?
_____

❺ Could you possible send me the report today?
_____

❻ Can you to clean up the meeting room?
_____

45.10 READ THE EMAIL THEN ANSWER THE QUESTIONS, SPEAKING OUT LOUD

What is Diego going to do?

> Diego is going to arrange the refreshments for the conference.

To: Gylfi Laarson

Subject: Conference preparations

Hello Gylfi,

Following our meeting yesterday, I have some more news about the plans for the sales conference. I spoke to Diego this morning about the refreshments and he's going to call ConCater Ltd today to make arrangements.

Sven is going to meet the printers about the posters and leaflets this afternoon. He's going to email us after the meeting when he has more news about prices. We need to move ahead ASAP on the printing.

I've emailed Diane and she's going to work on the Information Desk during the conference. Agnes is going to organize lanyards for all the delegates to wear. Could you arrange for the names to be printed for the lanyards, please?

I'm just going to email the venue to check that the rooms all have projectors and an internet connection. I'll email you later with a further update.

Best,
Simon

---

1 Who is Sven going to meet in the afternoon?

2 Who is going to work on the Information Desk?

3 Who is going to wear the lanyards during the conference?

4 What is Simon going to check when he emails the venue?

---

45 ✓ CHECKLIST

⚙ The future with "going to" ☐   **Aa** Polite requests ☐   🧩 Making arrangements and plans ☐

46 Vocabulary

46.1 FORMS OF COMMUNICATION

email

letter

envelope

stamp

internal mail

mail (US) / post (UK)

courier

delivery

telephone call / phone call

voicemail

answering machine

switchboard

transfer a call

text message

formal meeting

informal meeting

presentation

conference call

web conference

online chat

social networking

website

memo

bulletin board (US) / notice board (UK)

46.2 SENDING EMAILS

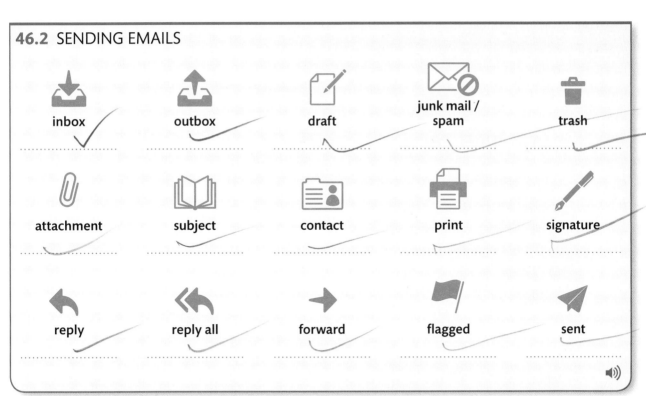

inbox ✓

outbox

draft

junk mail / spam

trash

attachment

subject

contact

print

signature

reply

reply all

forward

flagged

sent

46.3 ABBREVIATIONS

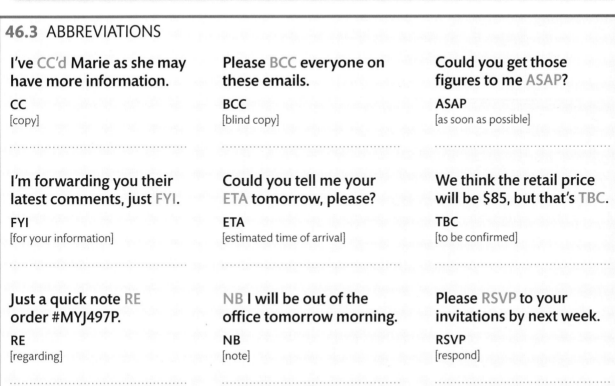

I've CC'd Marie as she may have more information.

CC
[copy]

Please BCC everyone on these emails.

BCC
[blind copy]

Could you get those figures to me ASAP?

ASAP
[as soon as possible]

I'm forwarding you their latest comments, just FYI.

FYI
[for your information]

Could you tell me your ETA tomorrow, please?

ETA
[estimated time of arrival]

We think the retail price will be $85, but that's TBC.

TBC
[to be confirmed]

Just a quick note RE order #MYJ497P.

RE
[regarding]

NB I will be out of the office tomorrow morning.

NB
[note]

Please RSVP to your invitations by next week.

RSVP
[respond]

Emailing a client

Emails to clients should be polite and clearly state your future plans and intentions. Use the present continuous or "going to" to discuss plans and arrangements.

New language Future tenses for plans
Aa Vocabulary Polite email language
New skill Emailing a client

47.1 KEY LANGUAGE EMAILS TO CLIENTS

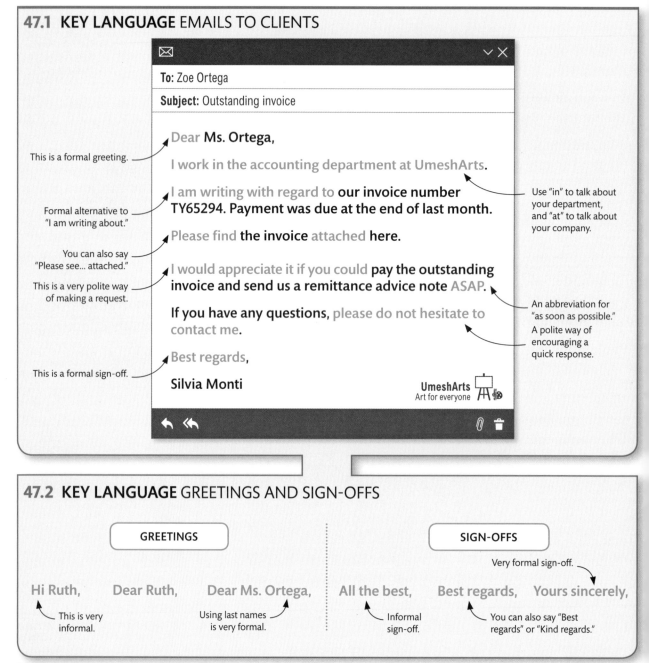

To: Zoe Ortega

Subject: Outstanding invoice

Dear **Ms. Ortega,**

I work in the accounting department at UmeshArts.

I am writing with regard to **our invoice number TY65294. Payment was due at the end of last month.**

Please find **the invoice** attached **here.**

I would appreciate it if you could **pay the outstanding invoice and send us a remittance advice note** ASAP.

If you have any questions, please do not hesitate to contact me.

Best regards,

Silvia Monti

UmeshArts
Art for everyone

This is a formal greeting.

Formal alternative to "I am writing about."

You can also say "Please see... attached."

This is a very polite way of making a request.

This is a formal sign-off.

Use "in" to talk about your department, and "at" to talk about your company.

An abbreviation for "as soon as possible." A polite way of encouraging a quick response.

47.2 KEY LANGUAGE GREETINGS AND SIGN-OFFS

GREETINGS

Hi Ruth,   Dear Ruth,   Dear Ms. Ortega,

This is very informal.

Using last names is very formal.

SIGN-OFFS

All the best,   Best regards,   Yours sincerely,

Very formal sign-off.

Informal sign-off.

You can also say "Best regards" or "Kind regards."

47.3 READ THE EMAIL AND ANSWER THE QUESTIONS

What is the main purpose of Zarifa's job?
Science ☐ **Recycling** ☐ **Technology** ☑

① What sort of companies does Zarifa work with?
Schools ☐ **Laboratories** ☐ **Technology** ☐

② Old microchips are currently being...
recycled ☐ **sold** ☐ **discarded to landfill** ☐

③ What does Science Solutions want to do with waste?
Purchase it ☐ **Discard it** ☐ **Sell it** ☐

④ What will benefit from this?
The environment ☐ **Science** ☐ **Nothing** ☐

⑤ How would Zarifa like to discuss further?
Email ☐ **Telephone** ☐ **In a meeting** ☐

To: Richard McGrath

Subject: Recycling opportunity

Dear Mr. McGrath,
I work in the recycling department at Science Solutions. I deal with repurposing waste from technology companies.

It has come to our attention that the microchips you no longer deem fit for purpose are being discarded to landfill. I wonder if you are aware that we could purchase this waste from you? Such a proposition would benefit both your company and the environment.

I would welcome the opportunity to discuss this further with you in a meeting.

Best regards,
Zarifa Sahli

Science Solutions

47.4 REWRITE THE SENTENCES, CORRECTING THE ERRORS

I am writing with regarding to your damaged packages.
I am writing with regard to your damaged packages.

① Please find your attached to invoice this email.

② I am writing to you as the new CEO in Yoghurt500.

③ I would am appreciate it if you could reply by 3 o'clock this afternoon.

④ My name's Scott and I work at the packaging department.

47.5 KEY LANGUAGE TALKING ABOUT FUTURE ARRANGEMENTS

To tell clients about future plans, you can use the present continuous, particularly if you have specified when something will happen.

I am writing to inform you that we are meeting other suppliers on Monday.

Present continuous.

We know when this will happen.

"Going to" can be used with a time marker, but it is often used instead of the present continuous to talk about plans for an unspecified time in the future.

I am writing to inform you that we are going to meet other microchip suppliers.

Future with "going to."

We don't know when this will happen.

47.6 CROSS OUT THE INCORRECT WORDS IN EACH SENTENCE

We are ~~paying~~ / going to pay your invoice very soon.

1. He is **emailing** / going to emailing all the clients this afternoon.

2. She is **to sending** / going to send vouchers to all customers.

3. They are **meet** / going to meet in Rome to discuss options.

4. I am **speaking** / going speaking with our couriers tomorrow.

47.7 FILL IN THE GAPS USING THE PHRASES IN THE PANEL

We _____ *are meeting* _____ our new clients on Friday.

1. We hope they're _____ us a discount.

2. Our CEO is _____ a merger.

3. Simone is _____ your invoice this afternoon.

4. Mark and Johan are _____ the calls later.

going to discuss

going to offer

~~are meeting~~

going to answer

sending

47.8 REWRITE THE HIGHLIGHTED PHRASES, CORRECTING THE ERRORS

> with regard to the

1 _____

2 _____

3 _____

4 _____

5 _____

6 _____

✉

To: Ian Grant

Subject: Agenda for meeting

Dear Mr. Grant,

I am writing with regard the annual meeting later this week. The meeting is going to taking place in the main boardroom of our Gold Road building at 1:00pm on Thursday. Please find attachment the agenda for the meeting. We is going to discuss the sales figures for the last quarter. Markos Kaloyiannis who works at the design department is also attend the meeting on Thursday. He is going discuss the design for the new coffee jars.

We look forward to seeing you there,

Kind regards,
Anton Schmidt

47 ✓ CHECKLIST

⚙ Future tenses for plans ☐   **Aa** Polite email language ☐   🧩 Emailing a client ☐

♻ REVIEW THE ENGLISH YOU HAVE LEARNED IN UNITS 42–47

NEW LANGUAGE	SAMPLE SENTENCE	☑	UNIT
INFORMAL PHONE CALLS	Can I ask who's calling, please? **I have to** hang up **now. I'll** call you back **later.**	☐	42.1, 42.10
FORMAL PHONE CALLS	Customer Service. How can I help you? May I ask who's calling?	☐	43.1
ADJECTIVE ORDER	**I've booked a** nice little **restaurant for lunch.**	☐	43.5
WRITING YOUR RÉSUMÉ	**I have a** proven track record **in sales.**	☐	44.1
FUTURE WITH "GOING TO"	**I am** going to **arrange a training course.**	☐	45.1
EMAILS TO CLIENTS	I am writing with regard to **our invoice number TY65294.**	☐	47.1
TALKING ABOUT FUTURE PLANS	We are meeting **other suppliers** on Monday.	☐	47.5

Answers

1.2 🔊
1. Hello. My **name's** Sebastian.
2. Good **afternoon**. My name is Joe Carr.
3. Hi, Marie. **I'm** Clive.
4. It's great to meet you, **too**, Sven.
5. It's a **pleasure** to meet you.

1.4
1 B 2 A 3 B 4 A 5 B

1.6 🔊
1. **It's a pleasure to meet you**, too.
2. Hi, **I'm** Adedeyo. / Hi, **my** name's Adedeyo.
3. **Great** to meet you.
4. This **is** my new colleague, Martin.
5. Marisa, **meet** Roula, my partner.
6. It's good to **meet you**, Katherine.
7. **May I** introduce Claudia Gomez, our new CEO?

1.7
1. Greene 2. 14 years 3. Accountant
4. Jill and Mr. Singh

1.8 🔊
1. Hello, Mr. Lucas. It's a **pleasure** to meet **you**.
2. Ashley, **meet** André. André and I work on the **same** project.
3. **Hello**, Sophie. My **name's** Rachel Davies. Great to meet you.
4. **This** is my colleague, Hayley. We went to college **together**.
5. It's **good** to meet you, Cori. **My** name's Angel.
6. Hello, James. **It's** really nice **to** meet you. My name's Alex.

2.4 🔊
1. He opens all the windows in the afternoon.
2. He brings the team tea and coffee every afternoon.
3. She shouts at the computer every day.
4. She walks around her office every 30 minutes.

2.5 🔊
1. She **is** a hairdresser.
2. He **travels** by train every morning.

3. She **leaves** work at 6pm every day.
4. She **drinks** coffee twice a day.
5. He **eats** lunch at a local café.

2.6
1. False 2. True 3. False
4. Not given 5. False

2.8 🔊
1. The head of marketing **speaks** for about an hour at every team meeting.
2. Arianna and Gabriel **read** their emails first thing every morning.
3. The photocopier **stops** working if we don't load the paper carefully.
4. The owners of the hotel **visit** it at the end of every month.
5. The cleaner **starts** work at 6am every day. The office is always clean in the mornings.

2.9 🔊
1. I work from Monday to Friday.
2. I have a meeting every morning.
3. You work from Monday to Friday.
4. You have a meeting every morning.
5. She works from Monday to Friday.
6. She has a meeting every morning.
7. My manager works from Monday to Friday.
8. My manager has a meeting every morning.

2.10
1. False 2. True 3. True 4. False
5. True 6. False 7. True

4.4 🔊
1. I'm on the **European** sales team.
2. Our **Chilean** office is in Santiago.
3. We sell leather shoes from **Spain**.
4. My job is to watch the **Asian** markets.
5. Book a trip to **Mexico** with us.

4.5
1. India 2. France 3. Asia
4. Italy 5. Africa

4.7 🔊
1. These polo shirts **aren't** made in Vietnam.
2. This restaurant **doesn't** use British meat.
3. The onions in this market **aren't** local.
4. **I'm not** Brazilian, but I work in Brazil.
5. The company **doesn't** have overseas clients.

4.9
1. True 2. False 3. True 4. False
5. False 6. True

6.3 🔊
1. Are the windows open?
2. Is your phone working?
3. Are these your files?
4. Is that drawer locked?
5. Is his desk clean?

6.6 🔊
1. **Does** he have a key for this drawer?
2. **Does** your laptop have a DVD drive?
3. **Do** Jim and Tom have new screens?
4. **Do** you keep pens in your desk drawer?
5. **Does** Sarah write the minutes?
6. **Do** all employees have wall calendars?

6.7
A 3 B 4 C 1 D 5 E 2

6.10 🔊
1. **Where** are the cups?
2. **What** is the photocopier code?
3. **How** do I turn off the screen?
4. **Why** is this drawer always locked?
5. **When** does the cafeteria open?
6. **Who** do I ask for printer ink?
7. **What** do you discuss at meetings?

6.11 🔊
1. You need to talk to Anne in HR.
2. It's always full on weekend evenings.
3. So that Marie can control the stock.
4. Turn it on and then select your drink.
5. At 2 o'clock. We usually start on time.

6.12 🔊
1. What can I do to help you?
2. Do you know where the key is?
3. When does the store open?
4. How do I connect the keyboard?
5. Why is her desk always a mess?

6.13 🔊
1. **Where** are the paperclips and pens?
2. **What** is for lunch today?
3. **Why** do we use old computers?
4. **When** do they close the office?

7.4
A 2 B 5 C 3 D 1 E 4 F 6

7.5 🔊
1. Do you **have** a website I can look up?
2. Your job **title** isn't listed here.

3 Just **drop** me a line for more details.
4 How can I **reach** you to follow up?
5 Is this your phone **number**?
6 Here's my **business** card.
7 **Call** me to arrange a meeting.
8 Drop me a **line** to follow up next week.

7.6
1 True **2** False **3** False **4** False
5 False **6** True

7.8 ◀))
1 Yes, it is. **2** Yes, they are. **3** Yes, they do.
4 Yes, it does. **5** No, we don't.

7.9 ◀))
1 No, it isn't. **2** Yes, they are. **3** Yes, I do.
4 No, it doesn't. **5** Yes, they do.
6 Yes, I do. **7** No, I don't.

08

8.4 ◀))
1 They **don't** have interviews today.
2 He **hasn't** got a diploma
3 I **don't have** any experience.
4 Do you **have** good IT skills?
5 We **have** monthly training sessions.
6 He **doesn't** have experience with animals.
7 He **has** a Master's degree.
8 They **have** a lot of inexperienced staff.
9 She's **got** super negotiation skills.

8.5
1 Sam loves working with animals.
2 Sam won a regional competition.
3 Sam organized field trips at college.
4 Sam worked in an office.
5 Sam has excellent photography skills.
6 Sam's degree is in dance and drama.
7 Sam has a photography diploma.

8.8 ◀))
1 Oh, yes. I know **the** hotel you mean.
2 Susan has **a** diploma.
3 Is **the** meeting on the second floor?
4 I work for **a** large recruitment agency.
5 There's **an** ad for a chef here.
6 I hired **a** PA to help me out.
7 He works at **the** hospital down the road.
8 Is there **an** office in Mexico?

8.9
A 4 **B** 1 **C** 5 **D** 2 **E** 6 **F** 3

8.11 ◀))
1 He was out of the office today.
2 I have excellent people skills.
3 What skills do you need for this job?

4 Have you read the job requirements?
5 She's an architect for a top company.
6 The new designer is very good.

8.12
Dear Mr. Baxter,
I am writing to apply for **the** role of Library
Assistant, which I saw advertised on your
website. I **have** two years' experience working
as a part-time assistant in my local library. **The**
job involves working with **a** team of people
and the public, so I have **good people skills**.
I **do not have** a degree in Library and
Information Studies, as **the** ad requested,
but I **have** a degree in English Literature.
I look forward to hearing from you.
Yours sincerely,
Judy Stein

10

10.4 ◀))
1 She **doesn't like** using computers.
2 He likes **training** new colleagues.
3 I **hate** long meetings.
4 We **don't like** lazy employees.
5 She enjoys **working** in a team.

10.5
1 Dislikes **2** Likes **3** Likes **4** Likes

10.6
1 False **2** True **3** False
4 False **5** True

11

11.3 ◀))
1 There **aren't** any bathrooms on this floor.
2 Is there **a** stationery cabinet in the office?
3 There's **a** staff cafeteria on the third floor.
4 There **isn't** an elevator in this building.
5 **Are** there any places to lock my bicycle here?
6 **Is** there a desk ready for our new designer?
7 **There are** lots of envelopes in the cabinet.

11.4 Model Answers
1 They should leave them in a closet by the
main entrance door.
2 There are four desks in Jonathan's office.
3 There is a tea and coffee machine.
4 Staff sign in at reception.

11.5 ◀))
1. There is a staff parking lot.
2. There is a business dress code.
3. There are places to relax.

4. There isn't a staff parking lot.
5. There isn't a business dress code.
6. There aren't any places to relax.

13

13.3
A 4 **B** 1 **C** 5 **D** 2 **E** 3

13.4
POSITIVE: **motivated, ambitious, helpful,
bright, intelligent**
NEGATIVE: **impatient, lazy, impolite,
nervous, boring**

13.5 ◀))
1 My team leader **is impolite** and he is also
very impatient.
2 My co-workers say that I **am really
motivated and ambitious**.
3 The new young intern seems very
intelligent and he **is really** polite.
4 I'm very lucky. All my colleagues **are**
hardworking and **helpful**.

13.9 ◀))
1 Two of the people on **my** team are new to
the company, but they're settling in well.
2 **Their** manager is very good with people.
They enjoy working with him.
3 The company is very proud of **its**
reputation and quality products.
4 Is this **your** phone? It doesn't belong to me
but I found it on my desk.

13.12 ◀))
1 We hate their product, but we love **ours**.
2 They are proud of **their** project.
3 **Our** clients expect excellent service.
4 This isn't her desk. It's **mine**.
5 This is amazing. Is it **her** project?

13.13 ◀))
1 I think these are your files.
2 Is this desk his?
3 These are her pens.
4 Are those products theirs?

13.16 ◀))
1 The **interns** work really hard.
2 All the team **members** are intelligent.
3 This big room is my **boss's** office.
4 All the **bosses** have parking spaces.
5 The best thing about this product is
its strength.

13.17
1 he joined the company
2 Jorge's supervisor

3 Her progress is slow
4 Maria is impatient
5 very intelligent

13.18 🔊

1. You are my manager.
2. You are my assistant.
3. You are Sam's manager.
4. You are Sam's assistant.
5. You are very organized.
6. You are really organized.
7. We are very organized.
8. We are really organized.
9. Katy is my manager.
10. Katy is Sam's manager.
11. Katy is my assistant.
12. Katy is Sam's assistant.
13. Katy is very organized.
14. Katy is really organized.

14

14.3 🔊

1 That meeting was really **boring**.
2 The printer can be **annoying** at times.
3 By the end of the week, I'm really **tired**.
4 The system is **confusing** at first.
5 I'm very **excited** about my project.
6 The news was **shocking**.
7 I was very **surprised** by my raise!

14.4

1 Not given 2 True 3 False
4 Not given 5 False

14.5 🔊

1 satisfied 2 bored 3 tired
4 confusing 5 annoying 6 interesting
7 excited 8 shocking

14.8 🔊

1 This printer is **faster** than the other, but that one is **more reliable**.
2 This coffee is **stronger** than I normally buy, but it is also **tastier**.
3 This building is **newer** than my last workplace, and the area is **quieter**.
4 This café is **busier** than the other one, so the service is **slower**.
5 My new uniform is **more comfortable** than my old one, but **uglier**.

14.10 🔊

1 Parking is more expensive this year.
2 This system is better than before.
3 I have more work to do than last year.
4 I arrive much earlier than my boss.
5 Every year my raise is smaller.
6 I feel better now that I have a new job.

7 A digital copy is more useful to me.
8 That meeting was worse than usual.

14.11

1 better salary 2 worse overtime pay
3 hourly rate is less 4 shorter commute
5 bigger bonus

14.12 🔊

1 easy 2 bored 3 stronger 4 lower
5 cheap 6 heavier 7 smaller 8 large
9 worse

14.13

1 friendlier 2 more successful 3 more
4 better 5 longer

14.14 🔊

1 Now, my vacations are longer **than they used to be**.
2 This new computer system is more **efficient than the old one**.
3 These presentations are making me more **bored than yesterday's**.
4 These new laptops are **lighter than the old ones**.
5 The cafeteria lunches are **tastier than restaurant meals**.

14.15

1 False 2 Not given 3 True 4 False
5 Not given 6 True 7 True

15

15.3 🔊

1 Lunch is served at noon.
2 Don't leave before Mr. Davies.
3 Never arrive after 9am.

15.5 🔊

1 Let your manager know if you need to go out **during** the day.
2 My boss is in meetings **for** about four hours every day.
3 I have been here **since** 5am this morning.
4 Do not leave the building **until** you have signed out.
5 The office is closed from Friday **to** Monday.

15.7 🔊

1 I go by metro.
2 Sometimes I ride my bike to work.
3 I go by train to work.
4 I normally go to work on foot.
5 Sometimes I take a taxi to work.
6 I take the bus.

15.8 🔊

1 I always **drive** to work.
2 It's usually quicker to **cycle**.
3 When it's sunny, we go on **foot**.
4 I don't like taking the **metro**.
5 I **walk** to work to stay fit.
6 I read a book when I go **by** train.
7 I **take** the bus when it rains.

15.9

Ⓐ 8 Ⓑ 1 Ⓒ 3 Ⓓ 7 Ⓔ 2 Ⓕ 5 Ⓖ 4 Ⓗ 6

17

17.2

1 frequently 2 sometimes
3 occasionally 4 never

17.3 🔊

1 I often do yoga in the evening.
2 We occasionally go to see a play.
3 She often listens to music at work.
4 I always take photos when I go on vacation.

17.8 🔊

1 This is the best book I've ever read.
2 The piano is the easiest instrument to play.
3 Yannick listens to the loudest music.
4 Shopping is the most expensive hobby I do.
5 That was the worst play I have ever seen.
6 Exercising is the most relaxing thing I do.
7 Let's eat at the closest restaurant.

17.9 🔊

1 The **most interesting** gallery I've been to is in Paris.
2 I've just finished the **worst** book I've ever read.
3 The **longest** hike I've ever done is 15km.
4 The **farthest** I've ever gone cycling is 50 miles.
5 I think that hiking is the **most exciting** hobby. .

18

18.4 🔊

1 I played soccer after work last night.
2 He didn't walk to work today.
3 I worked from 9 to 5 yesterday.
4 She lived in Paris for four years.
5 I talked to lots of people on my trip.

18.6 🔊

1 We **arrived** late, but our boss **didn't shout** at us.
2 I **washed** my car, but it **didn't look** clean.

3 I **watched** the film, but I **didn't enjoy** it.
4 It **stopped** raining, but then it **started** snowing.
5 I **didn't walk** to work, I **cycled**.

18.9 🔊
1 Did you play board games when you were young?
2 Did he cook some pasta for lunch?
3 Did she stay at home and watch TV last night?
4 Did they watch a scary movie at the movie theater?
5 Did they walk home from work together?

18.10
1 True **2** Not given **3** False **4** True
5 Not given

18.11 🔊
1 They visited a museum.
2 She listened to music.
3 He watched TV.
4 They cooked a meal.
5 They played a board game.

19

19.2 🔊
1 It's two thirty. / It's half past two.
2 It's ten forty-five. / It's (a) quarter to eleven.
3 It's seven. / It's seven o'clock.
4 It's three twenty-five. / It's twenty-five past three.
5 It's eight forty-three pm.

19.5
1 March **2** August **3** 2014 **4** May 12

20

20.4 🔊
1 When I was a gardener, I **spent** the majority of my time outside.
2 I **met** lots of famous people when I worked as a reporter.
3 Benjamin **went** to nearly 100 countries as a pilot.
4 In his last job, he **had** a dog as a partner.

20.5 🔊
1 As a police officer, I had a uniform.
2 I met lots of famous musicians.
3 I went to catering school.
4 I spent a lot of time in museums.

20.6
A 3 **B** 1 **C** 4 **D** 5 **E** 2

20.7 Model Answers
1 Sadim chose to study engineering in college.
2 Sadim thought his father would give him a good job in his company.
3 Sadim felt angry because he wanted a better job.
4 Sadim wrote to his father that he would look for another job.
5 His father said he could be CEO one day.
6 Sadim finally understood what hard work was like in different areas of the company.
7 Sadim's work experience taught him to respect all employees.
8 Sadim's father made him CEO five years ago.
9 Myra began working in the mailroom two months ago.

20.8 🔊
1 I **felt** really happy when I left college with a top degree.
2 My manager **said** that one day I could be CEO of the whole company.
3 My tutor **taught** me that it was important to check my own work.
4 I **made** my girlfriend a big cake to celebrate her new job.

20.9 🔊 Model Answers
1 I saw an ad for the job in the store window.
2 I felt very excited on my first day.
3 I chose the job because I wanted to work with customers.
4 I left my first job five years ago.
5 I left my first job because the hours were long.

21

21.3 🔊
1 We opened our tenth store two months **ago**.
2 The company **recently** merged with one of its competitors.
3 Jane Hunt opened the first Hunt Bags store **in** 1995.
4 A new CEO started working here **last** year.

21.4
A 2 **B** 3 **C** 5 **D** 1 **E** 4 **F** 6

21.5
Model Answers
1 Ahmed founded Cake & Crumb in 2003.
2 At first, he worked from the kitchen in his small apartment.
3 In the company's first year, sales remained steady.

4 The company opened its first store in 2005.
5 Cake & Crumb employed 2,000 bakers by 2010.
6 Two years ago, the company launched a catering service for children's parties.

21.7 🔊
1 The number of people going to festivals **went up** last year.
2 Fortunately, the cost of fuel for transportation **stabilized** recently.
3 In the really wet summer of 2010, sales of umbrellas **rose** a lot.
4 The number of people downloading music **stayed the same** last month.
5 The number of students earning MBAs **remained steady** last year.

21.8 🔊
1 **At** first, the value of the company **stayed** the same.
2 Marketing costs **increased** and sales also **rose**.
3 **Last** summer, umbrella sales **increased** because it was rainy.
4 The number of customers **decreased**, but profits **went** up.
5 Two years **ago**, we launched an online delivery service and our sales **rose**.

23

23.4
A 4 **B** 1 **C** 6 **D** 3 **E** 2 **F** 8 **G** 7 **H** 5

23.5 🔊
1 Sales **are increasing** at the moment, so we **are getting** a bigger bonus.
2 Fashions **are changing**, so we **are adapting** to new trends.
3 Travel costs **are rising** this year, so we **are calling** each other more instead.
4 Profits **are dropping**, so we **are cutting** costs in all areas of the business.
5 We **are selling** a lot to Asia, so we **are planning** to open an office there next year.
6 I can't believe you **are working** late. You **are missing** the staff party!
7 I **am waiting** for my interview to start, and I **am feeling** nervous.
8 The company **is losing** money, so we **are considering** a restructure.

23.8 🔊
1 Are they buying this?
2 Is it working now?
3 Are we selling that?
4 Are you meeting him?
5 Who are they promoting?

23.9 🔊
1 There is no hot water left.
2 That's Giorgio. He's a great speaker.
3 Yes, I'm running two workshops.
4 He's giving a presentation.
5 Yes, I think he is.
6 No, I'm on the bus at the moment.
7 No, it's out of toner. I'm refilling it now.

23.10 🔊
1 Is the company buying everyone new laptops?
2 Is Maria giving her first presentation at the moment?
3 Is Rakesh designing the packaging for the new gadget?
4 Are we all going to the team meeting now?
5 Are they trying to improve sales in North America?

23.12 🔊
1 I'm not coming to work tomorrow.
2 Are you meeting the team today?
3 I can't go. I'm not leaving until 8pm.
4 Are we coming back here next year?
5 Are you coming to the party later?
6 I'm not taking notes today. Are you?
7 I'm having lunch at noon tomorrow.
8 Are you going to Asia this winter?

23.13
1 For 10 days
2 Next Monday morning
3 In the bookstore

23.14 🔊
Model Answers
1 I'm meeting the HR team.
2 I'm going to Paris.
3 I'm traveling by train.
4 I'm getting home at 7.15pm.
5 I'm finishing at 3pm.
6 Monica is leaving work on Friday.

24

24.2
1 Impolite 2 Polite 3 Polite
4 Impolite 5 Impolite 6 Polite
7 Impolite

24.5 🔊
1 Sorry to **interrupt**, but my figures are different.
2 I'm not sure. What do you **think** about new outlets?
3 I'm sorry, but in my **opinion** they will sell well.

24.6
1 False 2 Not given 3 True
4 False 5 True

24.7 🔊
1 **take** the minutes, **review** the minutes
2 **read** the agenda, **work through** the agenda
3 **send** apologies, **announce** apologies
4 **take a** vote, **casting** vote
5 **opening** remarks, **closing** remarks

24.8 🔊
1 environment 2 reduce 3 reuse
4 waste 5 green 6 recycle
7 resources 8 footprint

24.9 🔊
1 Tim **sent** his apologies. He can't come.
2 Let's review our **environmental** strategy.
3 Let's work through the **agenda** quickly.
4 We should look at **reducing** our waste.
5 I'm sorry to **interrupt**, but I disagree.
6 What do you think **about** recycling?
7 Let's **take** a vote on the new policy.
8 The meeting chair has the **casting** vote.
9 I'm **sorry**, but I don't agree.
10 I think it's the best strategy. How **about** you?
11 I just have a few **closing** remarks.

25

25.2 🔊
1 So did I.
2 Me too.
3 So do I.
4 Me neither.
5 Nor did I.

25.3 🔊
1 I suppose you're right, but it was so long!
2 Nor did I. It was too difficult.
3 Yes, I agree. She is very friendly, too.
4 I suppose so, but they are expensive.
5 Me too. They're practical and cheap.
6 Neither did I. He was always moody.
7 So did I. The menu was excellent.

25.5 🔊
1 You could be **right**, but I think it's ugly.
2 I'm **afraid** we disagree about the price.
3 I'm **sorry**, but I don't agree, Jan.
4 I'm afraid I **disagree**. It's too expensive.
5 I'm sorry, Joe, but I don't agree **at all**.

25.6
1 Jeremy strongly disagrees with her.
2 Jeremy agrees with her.
3 Sian disagrees with him.
4 Jeremy strongly agrees with her.

25.7 🔊
1 Yes, I suppose **you're** right about the new design.
2 You **could** be right, but I need to do more research.
3 I'm sorry, but I don't **agree** at all with that comment.
4 I'm **afraid** I don't agree about this one issue.
5 I'm not **sure** about that, Sara. I don't like it.
6 I'm afraid I **totally** disagree. That will never work.

26

26.3 🔊
1 They locked themselves in the fridge.
2 He burned himself on the coffee machine.
3 Both of you, protect yourselves from the sun.
4 We booked ourselves on a fire safety course.
5 I fell and hurt myself on the wet floor.

26.4
1 Not given 2 False 3 True

26.5 🔊
1 assembly point 2 first aid kit
3 fire extinguisher 4 fire exit

26.6 🔊
1 She's cut **herself**. Get the first aid box.
2 They paid for it **themselves**.
3 The machine started **itself**.
4 Please take care of **yourselves**.
5 Make **yourself** aware of the fire exits.

27

27.3 🔊
1 Let's do more promotion on social media.
2 We could redesign the packaging for this product.
3 What about hiring a software consultant?

27.5 🔊
1 You should reset the router.
2 She should tell him before he sees it.
3 I should order some more.
4 We should throw away the food.
5 He should walk around the office.

27.7 🔊
1 I am **unable** to come in the morning. How about the afternoon?
2 I **misspell** words so often. Why don't we get an editor?

③ The machine isn't working. We should **disconnect** it.

④ Are you **unwell**? Why don't we call a doctor for you?

⑤ These tests are **impossible**. What about doing easier ones?

27.8
Ⓐ 4 Ⓑ 1 Ⓒ 2 Ⓓ 5 Ⓔ 3

27.9 ◀))
① Let's use our old system again. This new one is so **unfamiliar** and slow.

② How about changing the time so that more people are **able** to come.

③ Let's discuss the negative feedback from people who **disagree** with our plan.

④ What about explaining the delay to stop people from becoming so **impatient**.

⑤ I love conventions! It's so easy to **connect** with new people.

⑥ I have no idea how to write this report. It seems **impossible**!

28

28.2 ◀))
① To **start** this talk I will give an overall introduction to the project.

② **Second**, after the introduction, I'll describe our role in the project.

③ Next, we'll **explore** the benefits of this approach.

④ After **that**, we'll look at the possible difficulties we might have.

⑤ Then, to **finish** we'll look at what future research we can do.

⑥ Lastly, I will **answer** any questions that you have for me.

28.4
① False ② True ③ Not given

28.5 ◀))
① slide ② screen ③ projector
④ microphone ⑤ flipchart

28.7 ◀))
① I'm happy to answer any questions.
② So, we've covered the main issues.
③ Does anyone have any questions?
④ Would you like to ask anything?
⑤ In short, next year is important.

28.8
Ⓐ 3 Ⓑ 7 Ⓒ 4 Ⓓ 2 Ⓔ 5 Ⓕ 1 Ⓖ 6

28.9 ◀))
① In **short** we are very proud of our new products.

② I'd like to **begin** by looking back at past sales.

③ That's all I have to **say** about the advertising campaign.

④ Let's move **on** to talk about the packaging we've designed.

⑤ Does anyone **have** any questions for me?

29

29.2 ◀))
① It's a special one for fire safety.
② There's a nice café across the street.
③ We're meeting clients later this afternoon.
④ I have saved all the documents.

29.3 ◀))
① Is your stapler broken? You **can** use mine.
② She **doesn't have to** come to the training session. She did it last year.
③ You **have to** turn off the light if you're the last person to leave the office.
④ He **has to** test the fire alarm every Wednesday morning.
⑤ We **don't have to** wear a jacket and tie in the summer months.

29.4
① Not given ② False ③ True
④ True ⑤ False

29.8 ◀))
① Could you **tell** Jan to call me back?
② Could you **check** this report?
③ Would you mind **ordering** more pens?
④ Could you **mop** the floor, please?
⑤ Could you **come** to today's meeting?
⑥ Would you mind **calling** back later?
⑦ Would you mind **turning** the light off?
⑧ Could you **wash** these cups, please?
⑨ Could you **pass** around the reports?
⑩ Would you mind **booking** me a taxi?
⑪ Could you **show** our clients around?

29.9
① False ② False ③ True ④ True

29.10 ◀))
1. Could you book a meeting room?
2. Could you send Sam Davies an email?
3. Could you call our supplier?
4. Would you mind booking a meeting room?
5. Would you mind sending Sam Davies an email?
6. Would you mind calling our supplier?

31

31.4 ◀)) Note: Negative sentences can also use the long form "was not."
① Gabino **wasn't listening** during the team meeting this morning.

② The internet **wasn't working** all day yesterday. I had to call my clients.

③ Hannah and Luke **were talking** during the CEO's presentation.

④ I **was forgetting** to do everyday jobs, so I wrote a list.

⑤ I put you on a new team because you **were losing** sales.

31.5
Model Answers
① He wasn't answering important emails.
② He was leaving Maria to reply to all the sales enquiries.
③ The author's advice was to talk to the co-worker.
④ José was feeling tired after lunch every day.
⑤ He changed his diet so that he ate more salads and vegetables.
⑥ He was working until 5pm every day last week.

31.6
Ⓐ 5 Ⓑ 1 Ⓒ 3 Ⓓ 2 Ⓔ 4

31.7 ◀))
① Sales were improving. It was **a win-win** situation.

② It's a difficult task. We must think **outside** the box.

③ The team was throwing money **down** the drain.

④ Was your assistant **pulling** his weight today?

⑤ We were working with a lot of **red** tape.

⑥ Now we're all here, let's get **down** to business.

31.8 ◀))
① The elevator is out of order.
② The printer was going haywire yesterday.
③ Our sales fell last year. Now we're in the red.
④ I'm tied up with these difficult reports.

31.9 ◀))
Model Answers
① Gloria is designing packaging for a health tracker watch.

② The marketing department sends her lots of emails.

③ She doesn't get much work done because she's busy answering emails

④ Mark wants Gloria to take it easy.

⑤ Gloria has written to Faruk to ask for advice.

32

32.2 🔊
1 Don't worry. I have copies of them here.
2 No problem. It's Carson.
3 No need. The signal's always bad here.
4 That's OK. We can have coffee first.
5 Never mind. I've got myself another one.

32.3
1 Yes 2 Yes 3 Yes 4 Yes 5 No

32.4 🔊
1 I'm so **sorry** I was late for this morning's meeting.
2 I'm afraid that's not good **enough**. I want my money back.
3 I would like to **apologize** for the rudeness of our receptionist.
4 That's OK, but please make **sure** it doesn't happen again.

32.8 🔊
1 She **walked** into the room and saw that Clive **was practicing** his presentation.
2 I **was trying** to make an important point when someone's phone **started** to ring.
3 The printer **was working** fine when unfortunately the power **went** off.
4 He **opened** the door and saw that we **were listening** to his conversation.
5 We **were eating** lunch in the cafeteria when we **heard** the fire alarm.

32.9
1 False 2 True 3 False
4 Not given 5 True

33

33.3 🔊
1 Adrian **has made** three flower arrangements already today.
2 I **have started** work on the report, but I won't finish it tonight.
3 Leah **has cut** four people's hair so far this afternoon.
4 It's early. We **haven't spoken** to any customers yet.

33.4 🔊
1 I've **just** left work and it's very late.
2 We haven't shown this to the public **yet**.
3 Have you **just** started selling this product?
4 She hasn't done her training course **yet**.
5 They've **just** opened the store doors.

33.5
1 True 2 False 3 False 4 True

33.7 🔊
1 **We received** your order two hours ago and sent it about an hour ago.
2 I made all those pastries this morning and **I've sold** them all now.
3 **I started** painting Ms. Malone's living room at 7 today, but I haven't finished yet.
4 I emailed the clients yesterday but they **haven't** replied yet.

33.8
1 Some of his new co-workers
2 He had a meeting with his boss
3 She finished her research
4 A marketing conference
5 They both liked his talk

33.9 🔊
1 I **started** in January this year.
2 No, she **hasn't** yet.
3 Yes, I've **just** finished.
4 Not me. I **haven't** been in there.

34

34.4
Model Answers
1 She did not enjoy it.
2 No one responded to her phone calls.
3 The company will ensure every customer is given a second contact number.
4 There wasn't a vegetarian option in the hotel restaurant.
5 The hotel will offer vegetarian and vegan options.
6 The company has given Ms. Chang a voucher.

34.5 🔊
1 We will refund it to your credit card.
2 I'll take it back to the kitchen.
3 We'll replace them with bigger ones.
4 I'll talk to him about his bad attitude.
5 They'll be with you as soon as possible.

34.7 🔊
1 I'm afraid your order **won't** arrive today.
2 We'll **change** your appointment now.
3 I'll **talk** to my manager for you.
4 We'll **send** you a replacement tomorrow.
5 I **will** contact the courier about the delay.
6 I'll **ask** the chef to bring you a new meal.
7 Your delivery will **arrive** later today.

34.8
1 Will 2 Won't 3 Won't
4 Will 5 Will

34.9 🔊
1 I do **apologize**. We'll **replace** the broken part for you.
2 I'm **afraid** it **won't** arrive until Wednesday.
3 We'll **offer** you a **discount** on your next trip.

36

36.4 🔊
1 If you go to China for business, will you visit the Great Wall?
2 If I go to China on business, I won't have time to go sightseeing.
3 If we win the contract, we will go out to celebrate.
4 Will you arrange a taxi if we land late at the airport?
5 We won't get a discount if we don't book now.
6 If you have a lot of luggage, you will need a taxi.

36.5
1 by taxi
2 Business Class
3 a former colleague
4 to do some sightseeing
5 his passport details

36.9 🔊
1 When you book a transfer, a driver meets you.
2 Passengers get annoyed if the plane takes off late.
3 You can order a special meal if you're vegetarian.

36.10 🔊
1 If you buy food on the plane, it **is** quite expensive.
2 If you **are** in a group, it is often cheaper to go by taxi.
3 Will it be cheaper to **buy** a return ticket if I come back the same day?
4 When you book flights early, they **are** usually cheaper.
5 Traveling is boring if you **don't** have anything to do on the plane.

37

37.4 🔊
1 The venue is straight ahead and on **the** left.
2 Excuse **me**, do you where the gym is?
3 Sorry, did you **say** it's on the right?
4 Go straight ahead and **turn** left.

5 The bus stop is in front **of** the park.
6 Do you know the **way** to the post office?
7 The hotel is 50 feet ahead **on** the right.
8 Do you **know** the way to the hotel?
9 **Go** straight ahead and you'll see the sign.
10 The bus stop is directly opposite **the** bank.
11 Turn right at the **intersection**.

37.5 ◄))
1 Do you know how to get to Silver Street?
2 It's in front of the red building.
3 Don't take the first right. Take the second.
4 I'll meet you across from the hotel.
5 Go straight ahead and turn left at the lights.
6 The bank is next to the station.

37.6 ◄))
1 Sorry, did you say it's opposite the café?
2 Go straight ahead and turn right at the intersection.
3 Do you know how to get to the venue?
4 Go past the post office and it's on the left.

37.7
1 A **2** B **3** B **4** A **5** A

37.8 ◄))
1 Take the first **left**, and go **past** the hotel.
2 It's across from the hospital. Take the **second** right.
3 Go straight **ahead**. It's on the **corner**.
4 Take the first **right**, then **go** straight ahead.
5 Just go **straight** ahead and it's on the **left**.

38

38.4 ◄))
1 The rooms were cleaned this morning.
2 The key was left in the door.
3 The VIPs were met in the boardroom.
4 Flowers were put in the hotel foyer.

38.5 ◄))
1 The car was driven by a chauffeur.
2 The key was found by the guest.
3 They were shown around the conference venue.

38.6
A 4 **B** 1 **C** 3 **D** 2

38.7
1 False **2** True **3** True
4 False **5** False **6** True

38.8 ◄))
1 pick up **2** fall apart **3** turn on
4 check out **5** look around

38.9
A 2 **B** 4 **C** 5 **D** 1 **E** 3

38.10 ◄))
1 Breakfast **was served** in the main restaurant.
2 The rooms **were cleaned** every day.
3 The reservation **was made** by my assistant.
4 Yes. Very. They **were decorated** beautifully.

40

40.2 ◄))
1 Yes, we spoke on the phone.
2 Have you been to Mexico City before?
3 I'll let Mrs. Singh know that you're here.
4 Would you like some tea or coffee?
5 Did you have a good flight?
6 I've been looking forward to this visit.
7 It's great to meet you in person.
8 Did you have any trouble getting here?
9 Can I get you anything?

40.4 ◄))
1 Would you like **a** cup of tea?
2 Do you take **(any)** sugar?
3 Did you have **a** good trip?
4 Could I have **some** water, please?
5 Here are **some** details about the hotel.

40.5 ◄))
1 I didn't bring any luggage.
2 Did you have a good flight?
3 Do you need any help?
4 Would you like to meet the team?
5 There will be something to eat.
6 Can I get you anything to drink?
7 Please take a seat and wait here.

40.6
1 The evening before
2 A product launch
3 Social media and marketing

40.7 ◄))
1 The **keynote** speech will start at 10am.
2 The main **presenter** used a lot of slides.
3 The main sponsor will **launch** a new product.
4 Every attendee gets a **lanyard** and a name tag.
5 In a workshop the **delegates** get involved.
6 There are lots of **networking** opportunities.

40.8 ◄))
1 They have **some** free food and drinks.
2 Do you have **a** lanyard already?
3 I have **some** business cards to give people.
4 I'd like to see **some** interesting talks.

5 Are you going to **any** talks today?
6 Do you have **a** business card?
7 Are you staying in **a** hotel?
8 They don't have **any** drinks.
9 I'm giving **a** presentation today.

40.9
2

40.10 ◄))
1 It's Leo Smart. I haven't collected my **lanyard** yet.
2 Yes, here. Please take my **business card**.
3 Yes, and I went to an interesting **workshop** this morning.

41

41.2 ◄))
1 Would you like to see the dessert menu?
2 Could we have some sparkling water, please?
3 Could I have a receipt for this, please?

41.3 ◄))
1 The **reservation** was for six, but now there are only five.
2 Is there anything that you **recommend**?
3 Yes. I'm **allergic** to shellfish.
4 It's ok, **but** the food is a little bit cold.

41.5 ◄))
1 How much rice do you want?
2 I don't need more. There's enough here.
3 There are too many seats here.
4 There's not enough water.
5 $40 for a steak! That's too much.

41.6 ◄))
1 I've eaten **too** many chocolates.
2 How **many** glasses do we need?
3 There's too **much** sauce on this.
4 How **much** should we tip here?

41.7
1 True **2** True **3** False
4 True **5** Not given

42

42.2 ◄))
1 Hi, Karl. It's Katie **from** HR.
2 Hi. I'm **calling** about the Wi-Fi.
3 My client is here. I'd **better** be going.
4 Can I ask **who's** calling, please?
5 Is there **anything** else I can do for you?
6 Hello. Olga **speaking**.
7 No, thanks. That's **all**. Bye.

42.3
Ⓐ 2　Ⓑ 6　Ⓒ 4　Ⓓ 1　Ⓔ 5　Ⓕ 3

42.4 🔊
❶ Hi. Can I speak **to** Jacob, please?
❷ Hello, Sophie. **It's** Ahmed from sales.
❸ Could I **ask** who's calling, please?
❹ Hi. Adam **speaking**.
❺ It's Sandy **from** IT.
❻ Hi. **I'm calling** because the elevator is stuck.
❼ Bye then. **Speak** to you soon.
❽ Can I ask **who's calling**, please?

42.7
❶ 6057700930
❷ 03069990555
❸ 01632960042
❹ 01184962027
❺ 07700900844
❻ 03069690447
❼ 01632960177

42.8 🔊
❶ **Can** you call Martin at the office?
His number's 902-555-4349.
❷ You **can** call me on my cell phone any
time. My number's 03069 991332.
❸ Hi, it's Myra. **Can** you call me back?
My number's 07064 881206.
❹ **Would** you be able to call me back? I'm at
the office. My extension is 8762.
❺ If you **want** to contact Samuel later, his
number's 01632 960441.
❻ I've got a number for Hanna if you **want** to
contact her. It's 321-554-8933.

42.9
❶ A project selling shoes
❷ She cannot connect to the Wi-Fi
❸ Enter a different passcode
❹ GJ330XS
❺ He will fix it

42.12 🔊
❶ Anna, can I call you **back** later from
the office?
❷ Suzanna always takes ages to pick **up**
the phone.
❸ Ethan, I will get back **to** you later with
an answer.
❹ I'll put you **through** to Ivor now.
❺ If a customer is very rude, you can hang **up**.
❻ I'll find out the information and get **back**
to you.
❼ I'm busy now, Valeria, but I'll call **you**
back later.

42.13 🔊
❶ I'll put you through to Simone in sales.
❷ I will call you back later this afternoon.
❸ Sorry about that; we were just cut off.

42.14 🔊
❶ get cut off　❷ pick up
❸ speak up　❹ call you back
❺ breaking up　❻ get back to them

43

43.2 🔊
❶ Can you say that I'll arrive late?
❷ Could I speak to someone in sales?
❸ Can I leave a message for her?
❹ Certainly. I'll just put you through.
❺ I have a problem with an order.
❻ Hello. I wonder if you could help me.

43.3 🔊
❶ May I ask who's **calling**?
❷ I'll just **put** you through.
❸ I'm **afraid** he's away today.
❹ **How** can I help you?

43.4
❷

43.7 🔊
OPINION: **useful, awful**
SIZE: **large, tiny**
AGE: **antique, new**
COLOR: **blue, green**
MATERIAL: **wooden, glass**

43.8 🔊
❶ My boss has a **friendly large white** cat.
❷ My computer is a **huge old white** desktop
from 1995.
❸ We're marketing a **clever tiny new** watch
that helps keep you fit.
❹ Have you seen the **amazing tiny black**
briefcase she has?
❺ The meeting room has a **very large
modern** painting.

43.9
❶ False　❷ False　❸ Not given　❹ True
❺ False　❻ Not given

44

44.2 🔊
❶ Personal statement
❷ Career summary
❸ Professional achievements
❹ Education
❺ Interests
❻ References

44.3 🔊
❶ I am **fluent** in Japanese and Mandarin
Chinese.
❷ I have a great deal of **hands-on** experience
in the construction industry.
❸ I have an **in-depth** knowledge of hair-
coloring techniques.
❹ As an ex-car salesman, I have a **service-
oriented** background.
❺ I am a highly **motivated** librarian and
love reading.
❻ I am **proficient** in all major types of
accounting software.

44.5 🔊
❶ Our teams **collaborated** to create the
packaging design.
❷ We **established** a new headquarters
downtown.
❸ I **coordinated** a staff training day for
all departments.
❹ I **volunteered** for a charity and built
a classroom.
❺ I **negotiated** with all our suppliers and cut
costs by 15 percent.

44.6
❶ True　❷ True　❸ False
❹ Not given　❺ False

45

45.4 🔊
Note: Answers to ❶, ❷, and ❹ can also be
written in contracted form.
❶ They **are not going to** invest a lot of
money next year.
❷ He **is going to travel** by plane and then
taxi to the meeting.
❸ **Are** you **going to meet** with the suppliers
next week?
❹ We **are going to buy** the best quality
business cards we can.

45.5 🔊
❶ Make sure you have your passports.
❷ Can you let her know what happens?
❸ We should email the printers today.
❹ It's good to work with different people.
❺ He wants to spend more time playing golf.

45.6
Ⓐ 2　Ⓑ 1　Ⓒ 3　Ⓓ 5　Ⓔ 4

45.8 🔊
❶ Could you come to my office?
❷ Why don't we discuss this at the meeting?
❸ Can you tell me when it's finished, please?
❹ Could we move these files?

⑤ Could you send the design to the printers?
⑥ Can you help me with these figures, please?

45.9 🔊
① Can **you help** me move this cupboard?
② Could you **be** a little neater, please?
③ Can you **finish** the design soon, please?
④ Could **we** meet at 5 instead of 6?
⑤ Could you **possibly** send me the report today?
⑥ Can you **clean up** the meeting room?

45.10 🔊
Model Answers
① Sven is going to meet the printers in the afternoon.
② Diane is going to work on the Information Desk.
③ All the delegates are going to wear lanyards during the conference.
④ Simon is going to check that the rooms all have projectors and an internet connection.

47

47.3
① Technology
② Discarded to landfill
③ Purchase it
④ The environment
⑤ In a meeting

47.4 🔊
① Please find your **invoice attached to** this email.
② I am writing to you as the new CEO **at** Yogurt500.
③ I **would appreciate** it if you could reply by 3 o'clock this afternoon.
④ My name's Scott and I work **in** the packaging department.

47.6 🔊
① He is **emailing** all the clients this afternoon.
② She is **going to send** vouchers to all customers.

③ They are **going to meet** in Rome to discuss options.
④ I am **speaking** with our couriers tomorrow.

47.7 🔊
① We hope they're **going to offer** us a discount.
② Our CEO is **going to discuss** a merger.
③ Simone is **sending** your invoice this afternoon.
④ Mark and Johan are **going to answer** the calls later.

47.8
① is going to take place
② Please find attached
③ We are going to
④ in the
⑤ is also attending
⑥ going to discuss

Index

Subjects are indexed by unit number. Entries in **bold** indicate the unit with the most information.

Acknowledgments

The publisher would like to thank:
Amy Child, Dominic Clifford, Devika Khosla, and Priyansha Tuli for design assistance; Dominic Clifford and Hansa Babra for additional illustrations; Sam Atkinson, Vineetha Mokkil, Antara Moitra, Margaret Parrish, Nisha Shaw, and Rohan Sinha for editorial assistance; Elizabeth Wise for indexing; Jo Kent for additional text; Scarlett O'Hara, Georgina Palffy, and Helen Ridge for proofreading; Christine Stroyan for project management; ID Audio for audio recording and production; David Almond, Gillian Reid, and Jacqueline Street-Elkayam for production assistance.

DK would like to thank the following for their kind permission to use their photographs:
25 **Fotolia**: semisatch (center). 37 **Fotolia**: Leonid Smirnov (bottom center). 55 **Dorling Kindersley**: NASA (top right) All other images are copyright DK. For more information, please visit **www.dkimages.com**.